Industrial Britain

THE NEW SCOTLAND

Industrial Britain

THE NEW SCOTLAND

David Turnock

David & Charles

Newton Abbot London North Pomfret (Vt)

British Library Cataloguing in Publication Data

Turnock, David
  The new Scotland. - (Industrial Britain).
  1. Scotland - Industries   2. Scotland - Rural
  conditions
  I. Title   II. Series
  338'.09411   HC257.S4

  ISBN 0-7153-7560-1

Library of Congress Catalog Card Number 78 - 58561

FOR GRAHAM AND ANDREW

Printed in Great Britain
by Redwood Burn Limited
for David & Charles (Publishers) Limited
Brunel House Newton Abbot Devon

Published in the United States of America
by David & Charles Inc
North Pomfret Vermont 05053 USA

Contents

Preface

This book on the 'New Scotland' seeks to draw attention to the special characteristics of the Outer Regions of the country, which have been much affected by recent developments, especially the offshore oil industry. This project is somewhat unconventional because it attempts to combine two geographically separate peripheral areas, the North and South of Scotland. Since this means putting together such sharply contrasting areas as the Hebrides and Solway Plain, the formula may well appear to contradict tradition which would draw a clear distinction, with respect to both physical and human geography, between Highland and Lowland areas of Scotland. But while it is undeniable that the Highlands and Islands have certain very specific characteristics, it is argued here that the peripheral rural regions of Scotland have many common problems today. Whereas the Highlands and Islands was virtually the only major area of Scotland which failed to provide adequate new employment for its population during the eighteenth- and nineteenth-century modernisation of agriculture and industry, the last hundred years have seen the debilitating phenomenon of persistent heavy out-migration affecting all the Outer Regions. These areas exhibit a degree of coherence from their peripheral position in relation to Scotland's primary growth zone, the Central Belt.

The economic theory of growth poles may well be applied here to portray a highly industrialised axis, extending from the Ayrshire coalfield towards Tayside, virtually surrounded by an extensive hinterland supplying labour and raw materials in return for manufactured goods and special services. There is no space in this book to explore the theory in depth, but empirical evidence appears to justify such a dualistic view of Scotland, and post-war planning has been based on this reality. Thus the Scottish Plan of 1966 focused primarily on the Central Belt 'where the problems and possibilities of economic growth

exist at the largest scale' (p 37). The Outer Regions, covering
83.5 per cent of the area of Scotland, embraced only 26.5 per
cent of the population and 19.0 per cent of the employment in
manufacturing, due to the limited presence of many sectors which
had the dynamism and profitability to secure and maintain a
foothold in the Central Belt.

The economic strength of the Outer Regions in manufacturing
is relatively modest, but there is some merit in singling out
such an area for discussion. The industrial structure is not
just a scaled-down equivalent of the Central Belt. There is an
emphasis on such activities as food and timber processing,
showing close ties with primary industries. The aluminium
industry has a special significance in the Outer Regions due
to local resources, while the textile industry has a certain
coherence related to the uneven diffusion of new ideas and
technologies radiating from the Central Belt in the eighteenth
and nineteenth centuries. And in recent years the offshore
oil industry has brought a welcome diversification to the
industrial structure of parts of the North. Of course all this
is not to deny that each individual region in the group has
its own distinctive problems and potentials, and there is
certainly no suggestion of a clear separation of the Outer
Regions from the Central Belt. The Scottish Plan insisted that
each of the rural areas considered at the time by the Scottish
Economic Planning Council had 'sufficient consistency and
coherence to help sharpen the focus on local problems' (p 44),
and it was also stated that the emerging theme throughout the
Scottish Plan's strategy was 'the interdependence of the Outer
Regions and Central Scotland' (p 60). However this very interdependence implies some fundamental difference of situation.

The Outer Regions find their earliest expression officially
in the rural study areas investigated by the Scottish Economic
Planning Council: Highlands and Islands, North-east, Borders
and South-west. The North-east was subsequently divided to
separate the Aberdeen and Dundee areas, and the five regions
were then subjected to more sustained economic studies and
emerged as administrative regions in the 1975 reorganisation
of local government, effecting a modified implementation of
the Royal Commission proposals made in 1969. The problem of
definition has been 'solved' by adopting these official
boundaries, with the exception of the Highlands & Islands
region which includes not only the official area but the three
island authority areas (Orkney, Shetland and Western Isles),
and the Argyll & Bute district of Strathclyde region (the rest
of Strathclyde is combined for statistical purposes with the

Central, Fife and Lothian regions to comprise the Central Belt). It is acknowledged that the boundary question could be the subject of considerable research into different relevant criteria, but such an effort, which would have to take the whole of Scotland into account, would not really be justified in the present context.

However, it is appropriate to stress the ambivalence of some marginal areas. Argyll & Bute district is part of Strathclyde region and has clear functional ties with Glasgow, but it is included in the Highlands & Islands, to which region many of the inhabitants would like to belong because of close affinities with regard to social and economic structure as well as the Highlands and Islands Development Board's continuing interest in the area. The Tayside region is considered as one of the Outer Regions for the purposes of this book, but the area has been seen by planners as an extension of the Central Belt while the Borders, another Outer Region, has sometimes been seen as an extension of a region focusing on Edinburgh.

The various regional boundaries are shown in Fig 1 and the basic pattern is shown on all other maps which deal with the Outer Regions as a whole. Information for the Central Belt is not normally plotted in detail, except where the advantage of an all-Scotland view outweighs the drawbacks of cramming and additional research. In the Tables there is also an attempt to standardise the format with the regional figures supplemented by calculations for the North and South as well as for the Outer Regions as a whole and the Central Belt. Problems arise because the limits of the new administrative regions do not always coincide with the boundaries of the old counties. Regional statistics compiled from county information therefore assume the whole of Morayshire to fall in the Grampian region and the whole of Perthshire in the Tayside region, while Central Belt figures include the whole of Midlothian, although the southern part of this county is now in the Borders region. Tables using county figures are so designated, whereas on maps the inconsistency of the boundary lines can be shown directly. There is a further difficulty arising from the use of some of the old county names in the new district (second-tier) system, often with modified boundaries. Unless otherwise stated such names are always used to refer to the new district and not to the old county.

Limitations of space have prevented the full development of many themes introduced in the book. Those industries which are discussed in some detail have been selected on the grounds of their importance for the Outer Regions, if not for Scotland as a whole, and also because of the need for a documentation sufficiently adequate to sustain discussion of locational questions. But even so a number of leading activities have had to be omitted, with agriculture, forestry and fishing, along with related processing, as the most obvious casualties.

David Turnock
Leicester, March 1975

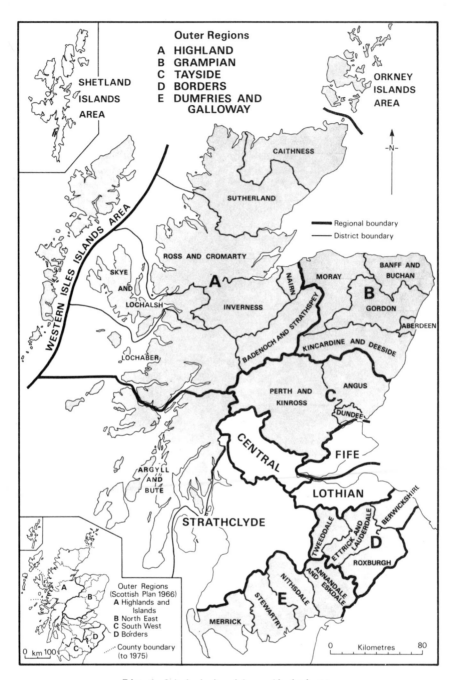

Fig 1 Administrative divisions

1

The Historical Base for Industrial Growth

Industrial development may be traced back to the imposition
of feudalism and the recognition of royal burghs which paid
taxes in return for important economic privileges and monopolies.
The more important royal burghs were in addition <u>caputs</u>
(centres) for their respective sheriffdoms, administrative
areas that were the forerunners of the counties or shires,[1]
and some enjoyed further distinction as cathedral towns,
Aberdeen and Elgin for example. But the distribution pattern
of the royal burghs was highly irregular outside the Central
Belt. In the North the failure to penetrate the Western
districts may be set against a surprising proliferation of
burghs around the inner Moray Firth, an indication, no doubt,
of unrest in the Moray province.[2] In the Grampian region the
alignment of royal burghs from Aberdeen through Kintore and
Inverurie to Fyvie and Banff underlines the importance of the
routeway passing between the medieval fiefs of Mar and Buchan;
and the curious elongated shape of the county of Banff,
preserved with only slight variations into modern times, may
be interpreted as a buffer between the loyal Aberdeen area and
the disaffected Moray province.[3] In the South the key route
centres were elevated to the status of royal burgh: Dumfires,
Annan Langholm, Selkirk and others. And in this zone there is
the interesting case of special rights of tenancy to farmers
in such strategically sensitive areas as the approaches to
Lochmaben Castle. For the vigorous defence of the triangle of
undulating land between the river and high ground, <u>kindlie</u>
(privileged) tenants were settled and their rights upheld
against feudal lords. As the late Arthur Geddes explains
'parliament must have been influenced by the stark need for
vigorous defence of this triangle; for in those hungry times
men would fight harder for the kingdom when they held landrights
to defend together'.[4]

Important though they were as strongholds and administrative centres, the policy of planting royal burghs throughout Scotland would hardly have been viable without the economic expansion experienced throughout Europe in the twelfth and thirteenth centuries. The Scottish burghs fostered trade not only at home but also with the continent, as witnessed by the scale of foreign settlement. This was considerable in the port towns right up to the Moray Firth, although a greater impact was probably made on Tayside. At Perth, where the river is just accessible to small seagoing craft, the original town probably spread along the line of the Kirkgait connecting kirk and castle; but in the twelfth century a much larger town was laid out, probably by the roughly simultaneous development of the High Gait and South Gait, taking building further back from the river. Perth became one of the leading burghs of Scotland and its system of parallel streets, thought to indicate continental influence, was shared by other towns in the Forth-Tay region. Berwick, further south, subjected for centuries to the rival claims of England and Scotland, was a flourishing woollen port with an important trade with Flanders.[5]

Industrial growth accelerated in the late fifteenth century, a period when the border quietened due to England's preoccupation with the Wars of the Roses.[6] Urban settlements grew and there was a flourishing trade with the Low Countries, France and the Baltic countries: the staple port of Campveere played an important role. More substantial, however, was the growth achieved during the seventeenth century, a period characterised by political stability, the discipline of Presbyterianism and an improvement of land transport with the beginning of the statute labour roads after 1610. Much of this upsurge worked to the benefit of the Central Belt. Glassmaking was first attempted at Wemyss in Fife. Coal and salt industries were concentrated in the Forth valley. The fine woollen industry, carefully stimulated until it succumbed to competition from south of the border after 1707, was closely tied to the Lothians, notably Haddington. Insecurity and inaccessibility of the Borders and Highlands helped to concentrate development in the Central Belt, but important exceptions arose from rich local minerals or other raw materials, adding a colonial appendage to the relatively developed core system. Non-ferrous ores were worked at Wanlockhead (Nithsdale) and close by at Leadhills (Lanark).[7] Local charcoal and bog ore supported an early seventeenth-century iron industry at Letterewe (Ross & Cromarty). Some 50 hectares of woodlands would have been felled each year and sent to the ironworks on the Furnace Burn near Letterewe House. Activity may have lasted half a century or

more, failing only with the exhaustion of accessible stocks of
timber. The domestic textile industry was gaining a high
reputation in some areas, notably the woollen stocking trade
of Aberdeen.[8] A more constructive Highland policy emerged in
the late sixteenth century: legislation against lawlessness
was followed by attempts to rationalise the landholding system
and provide some scope for royal initiative in industry and
land settlement.[9]

The Scottish Enlightenment

     The improvement of the country in the eighteenth century
was part of a European movement characterised by W. C.
Lehmann as a form of protest against a traditional theological
authoritarianism.[10] But in Scotland it had a strong national
flavour. It was not anti-religious; indeed the Presbyterian
Church backed the forces of change and made improvement a
virtue. Moreover the Scottish movement did not concentrate on
metaphysical questions but the application of empirical knowledge to public affairs, stimulated by the Union and the prospects of sustained economic development. Education was given a
very high value, and even before the mid-eighteenth century
many large parishes in the more developed areas of the country
had their parish school. Indeed, improvement in the widest
sense was the watchword of the day. There was a change in
society and also a change in the landscape. Large fields with
straight boundaries cut right across the old rigs and tracks,
planned villages were raised and estate mansions were shown off
by ornamental gardens. The very elaborate gardens of Castle
Kennedy and the terraces of Drumlanrig in Dumfries & Galloway
find echoes in the grandeur of Gordon Castle, the tasteful
plantations of the Glen of Drumtochty and the formal gardens
of Pitmeddan in the Grampian region. The ideas of improvement
in agriculture included the abolition of the run-rig system
and the consolidation of farm land. Land would be cleared,
drained, dyked and cultivated by means of an alternate system
of husbandry with the demanding cereal crops balanced by grass
and roots. The full bloom of the improving movement was achieved
from the 1750s, when rising agricultural prices coincided with
a period of great optimism for rural industry, to be carried
on in new village settlements.[11]

     At Grantown-on-Spey a village was laid out by the lairds
'to afford a permanent settlement to their ancient dependants
without driving them from the country, after it has been found
beneficial to enlarge the farms as much as possible'.[12]
Again, in the Banff & Buchan parish of Monquitter, the local
laird, Cumine of Auchry, decided to establish a permanent

14

market for the estate: 'for this purpose he planned a regular village contiguous to the church upon the moorish part of a farm',[13] because in this way good agricultural land would not be sacrificed and the village of Cuminestown would have the additional merit as a land improvement scheme bringing a substantial increase in rents. In Dumfries & Galloway there was the crescent-shaped spread of Garlieston (Merrick) begun in the 1780s and related, like the industrial village of Gatehouse of Fleet (Stewartry) begun in the 1760s, with the estate improvements of the Earls of Galloway. Equally notable is the case of Castle Douglas (Stewartry), rising out of a small estate situated close to Carlingwark Loch. Wide streets arranged on a grid-iron plan are characteristic of this small town of the 1790s. The settlement first named Carlingwark was built on the military road and attracted the local parish market from Rhonehouse on Keltonhill. Railway building confirmed the site as a central place with important stock-marketing functions. Another interesting example is Brydekirk (Annandale & Eskdale). This village was planned on a grandiose scale in about 1800 and the ambitious plans, which have survived, may be compared with the relatively modest achievements. The failure to implement the project for a new road from Langholm to Dumfries, in conjunction with which the village was con- ceived, limited the growth potential; but the close proximity to Annan and the declining importance of water power in the early nineteenth century were also significant factors. However, a small community lingers on in Brydekirk, 'a reminder of a landlord's hobby'.[14]

For most people in the Outer Regions, the improving movement must have been a period of great promise and excite- ment. The aristocracy had a monopoly of power, and this applied not only to their estates but also the smaller towns which remained virtually closed communities. Although we have no option but to accept the ministers' word, it may well be that 'the people were excited to industry by the prospect of enjoying what they acquired', and that 'they were taught morality by the most obvious argument that it afforded the best security for their persons and property'.[15] When the living conditions of the early eighteenth century are compared with the reports of increasing affluence in the Statistical Account, it would seem that a revolutionary change was opening up new opportunities for almost everyone. On the land a break was occurring between the principal tenants and the subtenants, for the dictum that 'a large farm is the only way of making estate by husbandry' made for reduction in the number of subtenancies.[16] But the demand for unskilled labour on the enlarged farms was considerable, and displaced tenants could

15

still find a useful role in society by moving to a village or
to a smallholding reclaimed from waste land. Unfortunately,
Highland experience disturbs this picture of steady progress:
although production was rising, conditions were highly variable
and better living standards had not spread far beyond the
fringes, as the waves of modernisation from Glasgow, Perth and
Inverness had only limited momentum.[17]

People in the Western Highland districts especially were
suffering growing hardship in the late eighteenth century, with
rising population pressure on limited land resources. It
proved difficult to introduce a viable commercial agriculture
because the physical conditions were unsuited to intensive
farming and the tenantry were unsympathetic to the new
methods.[18] Even cattle rearing was limited by the shortage of
low ground and shelted grazing, yet viable sheep farming would
require the removal of virtually all the native population. At
the same time other industries were slow to establish themselves: neither commercial fishing nor linen manufacture gained
any momentum in the remote districts, and this threw the whole
support for resettlement schemes on to the coastal muirlands
and other improvable lands where the crofting system was
introduced. As in the remoter parts of Ireland, public-works
projects rather than industrial developments were organised.
Although expected to bring economic growth in their wake, it
was to be found that improved communications were necessary
conditions of economic development, and thus they would not of
themselves stimulate growth without perception of a more
compelling economic potential.

Fig 2 summarises the highly variable progress made by the
improving movement in the late eighteenth century. Population
trends are remarkably diverse. The substanial falls in population in many Grampian and Dumfries & Galloway parishes indicate
strong local and regional migrations following improvement.
The towns of the Tayside area attracted migrants from the
Outer Regions, especially during years of famine, such as
1782-3. Many upland glens, Glenfernate (Perth & Kinross) for
example, experienced losses bringing to an end a burst of
population growth sustained by rising cattle prices and that
new subsistence crop, the potato.[19] But there was also the
flow of population to the Central Belt, which housed a
significantly larger proportion of Scotland's population in
1801 than in 1755. In the nineteenth century there was a
further demographic shift. The country was drawn into a single
economic system as never before, thanks to the solid peace
established in the Highlands and the remarkable improvements
in communication: roads, canals, steamers and railways.[20]

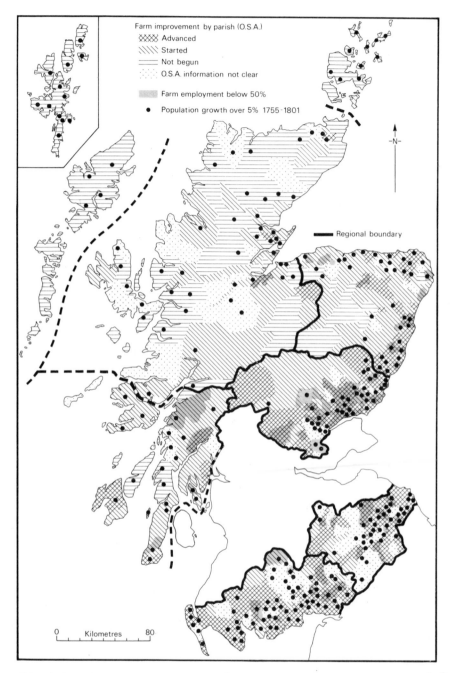

Farm improvement by parish (O.S.A.)
- XXXX Advanced
- \\\\ Started
- ——— Not begun
- ░░░ O.S.A. information not clear

- ▥ Farm employment below 50%
- ● Population growth over 5% 1755-1801

-N-

━━━ Regional boundary

0 Kilometres 80

Fig 2 The improving movement (Beauties of Scotland and OSA)

'Coal meant concentration': not only did metallurgy have a
strong link with the coalfields by virtue of the 'black-band'
ironstone as well as the 'splint coal', but the textile
industry (which had shown a surprising capacity to 'spread'
across the country, picking out areas with inherited skills or
water-power endowments) now tended to consolidate.

The Nineteenth and Early Twentieth Centuries

An examination of population trends reveals a growing
demographic imbalance between the Central Belt and the Outer
Regions.[21] Compared with a share of 57.8 per cent in 1801 and
46.8 per cent in 1851, the Outer Regions accommodated only
33.3 per cent in 1901 and 26.5 per cent in 1971. All the Outer
Regions show an absolute increase in population during the
first half of the nineteenth century, but during the following
fifty years the Highland Region and Dumfries & Galloway
register a net decline. The continued expansion in the other
regions is due almost entirely to the dynamism of the main
towns and cities. Only in the Western Isles is there evidence
of a general expansion of rural population. During the
present century, the degree of stability is very largely a
function of the growth of the burghs and their capacity to
absorb the migrants from the rural districts. In all the Outer
Regions the proportion of the population resident in the burghs
has grown progressively since 1851, but growth has not always
been impressive in absolute terms (the combined burghal
population of the Borders was less in 1971 than in 1901!) and
the percentage shares vary considerably between regions.

So, running in parallel with the great improvement in
mobility was an increased sophistication in the central-place
hierarchy. The rail services and their connecting coach routes
brought large areas within reach of the main cities on a day-
return basis. This strengthened the regional functions of
Aberdeen, Dundee and Perth. During the nineteenth century,
expansion in the burghs was largely an expression of industrial
progress. The cities of Aberdeen and Dundee entered the industrial revolution with the tremendous advantage of status and
privilege, large populations and port facilities. Although
distant from the coalfields, indigenous skills in industry and
commerce ensured the retention of a vigorous light industry,
especially evident in textiles, and built up a demand sufficient
to warrant local foundry and engineering industries. But other
towns display an ample Victorian legacy. At Hawick (Roxburgh),
where the first stocking frame was introduced in 1771 to pave
the way for a sustained nineteenth-century woollen industry

based on water-powered factories lining the Tweed and Slitrig, contemporary town planning and embellishment has left its mark. The urban fabric is dominated in the centre by the town hall of 1886, raised in the characteristic baronial style, but the offices of the major banks display an appropriate nobility. The influx of new workers brought a rash of tenemented buildings on rising ground on both sides of the Teviot while the railway, bringing welcome consignments of Lothian coal to solve the fuel crisis, made a bold architectural and morphological contribution, sadly represented today in an abandoned trackbed and decaying station buildings.

The uneven spread of industry was reflected in considerable irregularities in the central-place hierarchy. In the Grampian region (apart from the county of Moray), Aberdeen was unchallenged as the leading centre, but R. Paddison has demonstrated that it was the coastal settlements of Buckie, Peterhead and Fraserburgh that were the main secondary centres before World War II, largely due to the strength of the local fishing industry.[22] Such an arrangement was less than satisfactory from a welfare point of view because it left many inland areas a long way from towns with a good range of services. The upland areas of the Gordon, Kincardine & Deeside and Moray districts were poorly served even for third-grade centres. Such anomalies were common in the Highlands and reached their most exaggerated form in the islands where even the secondary centres were often well beyond daily commuting distance and, therefore, visited very occasionally. Relative isolation from the higher-order sevices has in the present century become increasingly intolerable to the younger generation, and although there may be compensations in the quality of the outdoor recreation in remote rural areas, lack of modern amenities is a potent factor in the decision to migrate. In the Borders, L. J. Evenden has examined the 'dispersed city' character of the Middle Tweed, with services largely geared to the needs of the burghs themselves, and contrasts the situation with provision in Berwickshire where agricultural communities have supported only such lower-order centres as Duns, which nevertheless have great difficulty in maintaining their position through decline in the rural population.[23]

Thus the legacy of the nineteenth century is expressed in urban patterns by gross inequalities in the spacing of the major centres.[24] While sparsely settled areas are bound to be generally more remote from higher-order services, distortions have arisen from variations in industrial growth. This is significant because only the larger burghs are likely to stand as attractive locations for new light industry, while distance

from services and employment opportunities increases the
feeling of remoteness in rural areas, stimulating emigration
even though local employment may be available. In the first
half of the nineteenth century there were many rural parishes
increasing their population and a few, such as Gairloch (Ross
& Cromarty), Kilchoman (Argyll) and Lochs (Outer Hebrides)
actually doubled their population in fifty years. But upland
districts accessible to the Central Belt show many declining
parishes, especially in Argyll, Perth and Roxburgh. The second
half of the century shows rural decline as an almost universal
phenomenon in the Outer Regions, some Argyll parishes losing
half their population. Only in parts of Banff & Buchan and the
Outer Hebrides is a net rural growth registered, thanks to the
continued expansion of agriculture, fishing and rural industry.
[25] During the twentieth century, rural depopulation emerges
again as the dominant theme in parish trends. Growth parishes
are largely restricted to the major commuting areas (Fig 3).
But it is evident that in Dumfries & Galloway very steep rural
depopulation has been avoided. With barely half the region's
population in the burghs, it is remarkable that the overall
population loss since 1901 has been less than 2,000. As a
popular area for retirement, with a relatively intensive
agriculture and an expanding forestry programme, rural decline
has been moderated.

     The railways eased the power-supply situation for
industry by aiding the movement of coal, especially beneficial
for the Borders, but this factor was only a significant benefit
if the industry was competitive in the newly accessible
markets.[26] Manufacturing in the Outer Regions generally lacked
the necessary physical and human resources and the scale of
production to provide effective competition. But for the
primary sector it was a very different situation. Livestock
could be delivered to distant markets in good condition or,
alternatively, an export trade in dead meat could be developed.
The success of the Aberdeen butchers is significant here, a
success which underpinned the new slaughter-house opened in the
city in 1909. In the North Isles there was now a stimulus to
complete the long-delayed agricultural reorganisation: in
Orkney small stock-rearing farms emerged from a consolidation
(planking) of farmland and a big increase in the area cultivated.
The steamship was also a 'wonderful stimulus' to the stock-
farmers of Caithness, whose 'spirited exertions' did much to
improve breeding.[27] The railways helped the dairy farmer in
Dumfries & Galloway by providing access to city markets which
were being denied their local supplies on account of stiffer
health regulations. They also assisted the arable farmer by
improving the supply of fertiliser and transporting harvested

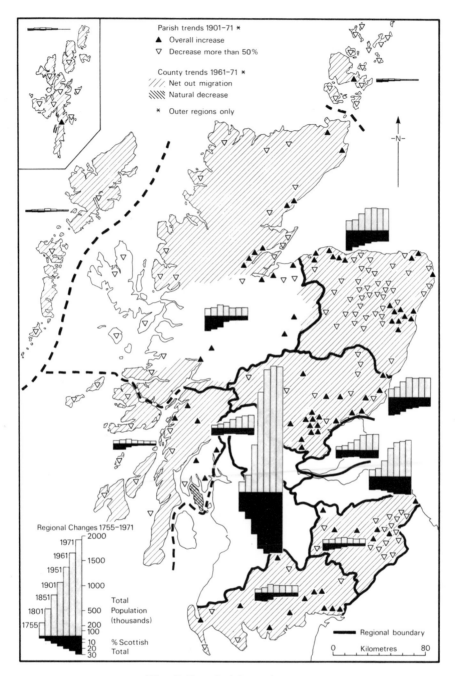

Parish trends 1901–71 *
▲ Overall increase
▽ Decrease more than 50%

County trends 1961–71 *
⫽⫽ Net out migration
⫼⫼ Natural decrease

* Outer regions only

—N→

Regional Changes 1755–1971

2000
1971
1500
1961
1951
1000
1901
1851
Total
1801 — 500 Population
200 (thousands)
1755 100
10 % Scottish
20 Total
30

Regional boundary

0   Kilometres   80

Fig 3 Population changes

crops; notably the potato grower, who had previously used his crop on the farm as cattle feed, and the soft fruit producers, who had previously been unable to compete with the Clyde Valley growers, felt the benefit.

New opportunities strengthened the smallholder. Planned villages had failed to retain their industries, and estate policy came to look more favourably at the establishment of moorland crofts where land could be maintained by artificial fertiliser and geared to produce store cattle required by the fattening units. A succession of good years in the 1850s gave further impetus to what became a farming mania when it seemed the four-course rotation would be taken right over the hill. But hungry soils and falling prices brought the speculation to a halt, and the sad legacy of the improving movement's last fling can be seen only too plainly in the ruined farmsteads of the Braes of Glenlivet and the lower slopes of Ben Rinnes (Moray). Yet the agricultural depression did not bring about an immediate loss of confidence. Coming hard on the heels of the 'golden age' and further expansion of the agricultural area, it was difficult to accept the setback as anything more than a temporary adversity. Besides there were few alternative avenues of employment open to the average country dweller. The Highland crofter was actually to reinforce his position as a result of the late nineteenth-century depression. This was due to a coincidence in timing between the depression in commercial farming and the protest movement by crofters. A Royal Commission was appointed under Lord Napier to look into the crofters' grievances.[28] The outcome was an act of parliament in 1886 conferring a large measure of security on Highland crofts. But it was largely thanks to the depressed state of hill farming that this first step could be followed up in the 1890s by enlargements of crofts and whole land-settlement schemes in the most congested districts. It was a limited recognition by government of the rural problems of Scotland, but because of an arbitrary decision to limit assistance to the Highland counties (or 'Crofting Counties'), there was no benefit for other regions; and in the Highlands the lack of a sustained rural programme eroded the value of the statutory privileges.

Also very important for the Outer Regions were the improved prospects for forestry, fishing and tourism Previously, charcoal industries in the West Highlands attracted iron smelters, of which Furnace and Taynuilt (Argyll & Bute) were the most important, while the floating of timber from Badenoch down the Spey to Garmouth tied in with a shipbuilding industry which was still important in 1850. But in areas like the upper

Don valley, where rafting of timber to coastal mills had never been feasible, it was the branch railway that provided the first real incentive for commercial forestry.[29] However, until the post-war developments in chipboard and pulp manufacture, the wood-processing sector dwindled to little more than small-scale sawmilling at such water-power sites as Glen Mill on Cargen Water near Lochrutton, and Kingan's Mill at New Abbey (Nithsdale). The Aberdeen sawmilling and paper industry is an important exception.[30] For the Highland fishing industry the railway access to the fresh-fish markets of the south was a benefit, although the attraction of the railheads dealt a severe blow to the island processing. The railways made a decisive impact on the tourist industry, opening up the Highlands to Victorian travellers who found their way to the deer forests and grouse moors as well as the spas and coastal stations. On Upper Deeside, upper-class patronage paved the way for realisation of the sporting and recreational potential of the area as a supplement to the farming and forestry, for which a narrow-gauge extension of the Ballater branch had been contemplated. The spa of Strathpeffer (Ross & Cromarty) won its branch line from Dingwall, and the fine hotel built by the Great North of Scotland Railway at Cruden Bay (Banff & Buchan) was connected with the company's Boddam branch by a light electric tramway. Contemporary guidebooks and other sources give a useful insight into the activities of Victorian visitors who built an industry which has proved to be of permanent value to the Outer Regions.

But in general it was a tragedy for the Outer Regions that the industrial opportunities available in the eighteenth century were to become gradually more elusive. With few viable alternatives to primary industries, the migration process was accelerated and only in recent years has industrialisation been accepted once again as a realistic policy for rural problems. Even before the superiority of steam power had been demonstrated the distribution of industry was highly uneven. Shortage of fuel prevented expansion in many areas, and this problem was only gradually solved by improved roads; but the advantages of the turnpikes were not always far reaching. It was said of the Dundee-Meigle turnpike that 'such as live near the turnpike and have easy access to it feel its great advantage and readily acknowledge it; while those who live at a distance derive but little benefit from it owing to the wretched state of the bye-roads which the commuted statute labour will never render tolerable'.[31] Moreover, water-power resources were very localised.[32] At Sanquhar, where the woollen-cloth, carpet and stocking industries are mentioned, the town enjoyed 'an unrivalled situation where there is plenty of water and descent to drive weighty machinery'.[33] But such examples are few in number. Where water power did not exist, wind might be a viable alternative, and even in well-endowed areas windmills could be a valuable supplement during periods of drought. Those mills near the towns, including Aberdeen, Dundee and Peterhead, were corn mills, as were the small farm mills in Orkney, while those at Spynie (Moray) and Strathbeg (Banff & Buchan) were used in conjunction with drainage projects. However, wind power proved too unreliable to use on a large scale, and by the mid-nineteenth century only a few mills remained at work.[34]

The Outer Regions failed to attract substantial investment in the most dynamic and profitable industries, since these activities could capture the most desirable sites near both coal and markets, but they do nevertheless possess their own industrial geography which, despite its vastly different scale from that of the Central Belt, has great interest because first of all it is possible to trace what has been described as the fossilisation of the 'rural-industrial' growth sparked off by the investments of landowners who drew their wealth largely from the cattle trade. There were numerous corn mills and drying kilns, many of the former being driven by water power. Breweries and distilleries were common: the Moray district and the island of Islay (Argyll) emerged as major producers of malt whisky by the end of the century. Tanning and leatherworking were natural activities in cattle country. But unlike the malt-whisky industry, which retains a strong link with the Outer Regions by virtue of its demand for peaty water, the leather trade has gravitated towards the cities. Some industries were successful in achieving and then maintaining a large scale of operation, at any rate in selected parts of the country. Quarrying is one such case. In the early nineteenth century this embraced the slate quarrying of Ballachulish (Lochaber) and Easdale (Argyll & Bute), the limeworks of Closeburn (Nithsdale) and Dufftown (Moray), and the granite of Aberdeen, Kemnay (Gordon) and Peterhead (Banff & Buchan). The greatest success in industrial development came with textile manufacture. The cotton industry proved disappointing, since initiatives in Aberdeen and Stewartry failed to take a permanent hold, but the linen industry, although unable to retain its rural locations in Dumfries & Galloway and the Highlands, did take a firm hold in Tayside, and the greatest success story in woollen manufacture must be told in the Borders where both tweed and hosiery are produced.

24

Economic Regions

    A fairly complete picture of Scottish industry in the late
1930s emerges from a survey undertaken by C. A. Oakley for the
Scottish Development Council.[35] The regional organisation of
his book makes it ideal for some assessment of areal differences
in the Outer Regions. 'Intense pride and independence of spirit'
characterise the Border tweed industry with numerous separate
production units. The rebuilt Ladhope Mill in Galashiels,
opened in 1930, was a well-equipped spinning mill and a sign
of confidence in the business, although some co-operation for
marketing was to be expected. The firm of Ballantyne Brothers
reorganised their works in 1937, confining spinning to
Innerleithen and weaving to Peebles. In response to foreign
quota restrictions, tweed firms were switching to worsted and
lighter tweeds suitable for women's clothing, some fabrics
being produced by arrangement with continental firms. The
Scottish Woollen Technical College in Galashiels was an
important part of the industry's infrastructure. Diversification
in the textile industry included a growing emphasis on hosiery
and knitwear: the growing demand for knitted outerwear was
sustained by Border firms whose unshrinkable garments reflected
a constant attention to fashion changes. This brought prosperity
to Hawick and also to Dumfries, where the Wolsey hosiery works
of 1912 was extended in 1931 and 1934 and where a second works,
for gloves and stockings, was opened in 1926. Another sign of
diversification was the beginning of silk weaving, using
Italian silk spun in England, in Galashiels in 1932. This
enterprise, supplying material for ties, linings and dress
facings, came three years after the North British Rayon Company
started making artificial silk in Jedburgh. Dyeing and finishing
remained important in Galashiels and Hawick, while new
capacity was provided at Dumfries, at the Troqueer Mills in
1929. But while the leading towns of the Borders were seeing
their female labour catchments exploited, notably at Dumfries
and Jedburgh, opportunities for men were limited. Engineering
firms dealing with agricultural and textile machinery in the
South were small, although boiler making was introduced to
Annan in 1889 and the closure of the Arrol Johnston automobile
factory was followed by the prospect of the premises being
taken over, in 1936, for aero and marine engines. Dumfries was
regarded as the only town in the South likely to show an
appreciable growth of population, thanks to its textile,
engineering and tourist potential. The employment problems of
the smaller burghs were eased only by the dairies of the
Scottish Milk Marketing Board (Fig 4) and a substantial bacon
factory at Thornhill.

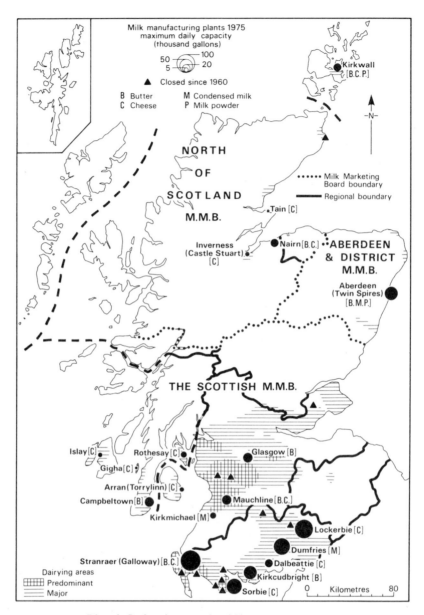

Fig 4 Dairying and milk manufacture

The Tayside area was another traditional centre of textiles, with the emphasis on the jute and heavy-linen trades that had suffered considerably since World War I. Specialisation in particular types of cloth was becoming characteristic, and fortunes varied between one trade and another. The carpet business was relatively buoyant, since research had made for improvements such as durability of colour and attractive design. Research suggested the practicability of waterproofing material to yield a non-cracking substitute for oilcloth and the use of jute cloth in roadmaking was also being considered. New floorcloth factories had opened by Kingsway, the new ring road in Dundee. Even spinning was being geared to particular grades and modernisation had begun, notably in the new Eagle Mills, incorporating high-speed machinery. Meanwhile, the jute industry was flourishing in Alyth, Blairgowrie, Coupar Angus and Kirriemuir, and heavy linen featured in Arbroath, Brechin and Montrose. Offering some alternative to the textile industry was engineering, concentrated in Dundee/Monifieth and shipbuilding and jute machinery at Arbroath/Carnoustie, where a similar bias towards heavy machinery for the jute and stone industries was combined with a trend towards lighter consumer items. Food preserving was notable as a growing light industry. In addition to the long-established preserving industry of Dundee were the canning plants of Blairgowrie, Brechin and Montrose which opened between 1926 and 1933, most of the capacity being owned by the major British companies attracted North by the excellent raspberry crop and to a lesser extent by the fish which was handled in one new Dundee factory. Another important development was the Camperdown Bitumen Refinery started in 1930. Although much of the liquid bitumen was shipped off to a variety of distribution points in the country, much is consumed in Dundee for tar manufacture and for impregnating jute cloth for use as roof and floor felts. Permanent roofing felt was meeting rising demand, justifying well-equipped premises in Dundee for its manufacture. Yet diversification still remained a pressing problem, and it was clear that better road transport would assist the search for new industry: although Kingsway had opened up new attractive sites for industry within Dundee, the indirect road communications with the South added support to the case for the Forth and Tay road bridges. Perth's more direct rail and road communications, and its potential as a centre for air transport in Scotland, sustained the whisky blending and chemical-glassware industry, supplementing the older textile and dyeing industries.

Aberdeen was left with a much-reduced textile industry

embracing the heavy linen, heavy tweed overcoating, hosiery and knitwear. But the paper industry, which originally had close associations with textiles, remained very prominent. Innovations in the paper industry included the improved production of newsprint, waterproof papers, art paper and business papers, respective specialities of the four Donside works, while at Culter, on a tributary of the Dee, the oldest continuously running paper mill in Scotland was turning out coated paper. And a substantial engineering industry persisted. The shipyards found a steady market for tugs and dredgers which diversified production away from the fishing trawlers and the small cargo steamers built at the close of the famous tea-clipper era. Mechanical-handling appliances, diesel engines and equipment for the agriculture, granite and paper industries concerned other engineering firms. The granite industry survived in Aberdeen: the pneumatic drill represented an important break-through in stone cutting, the memorial trade remained important and granite chippings were in demand from the roadbuilders and concrete pipemakers. Fish was a notable growth industry (Fig 5): concentrating on white fish, the depression of the herring ports was avoided; but improved efficiency was necessary to gain full advantage of the relative proximity to the fishing grounds, combined with rail transport to southern markets. It was also necessary for Aberdeen to decide on an enlargement of the fleet to extend the range of operations from the Orkney and Shetland banks to Iceland. The industry had a strong research effort behind it in the Marine Laboratory and Research Station, opened in Torry in 1920 and 1929 respectively. And the processing industry, including filleting, canning, curing and meal production was technically up to date. Finally, support to the farming community comes through the feed and fertiliser of Scottish Agricultural Industries formed in 1929 as an amalgamation of local firms from Aberdeen and Dyce. Elsewhere in the Grampian region industry was scattered, but a number of the small burghs retained a modest interest in manufacturing. The machine-knitting works of Wm Spence in Huntly (Gordon) represents a modern factory phase in an industry started in the late eighteenth century on the basis of outworkers in farms in the district. The same firm operated at Inverurie while two other inland towns, Elgin and Keith, had extended and modernised woollen mills, diversifying their tweed production with woollen scarves employing attractive colour schemes. The basic agriculture and fishing industries supported a significant manufacturing sector: the distilleries were expanding and fish processing was important, particularly in Fraserburgh and Peterhead (Banff & Buchan), the Fraserburgh plant originating in 1883. The relatively large coastal towns

28

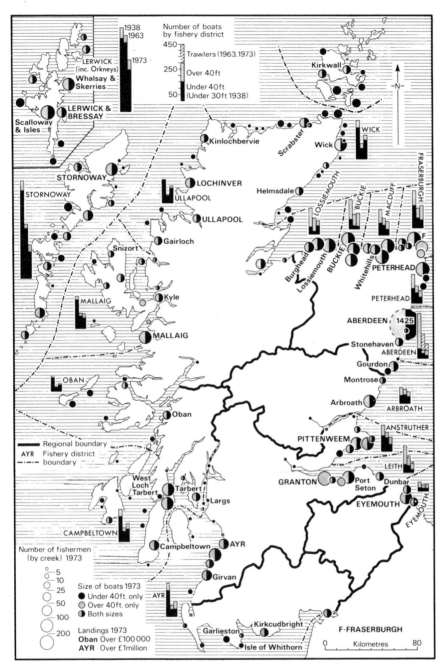

Fig 5 Commercial fishing 1973
(Scottish Sea Fishing Statistical Tables)

were beginning to attract heavier industries: the pneumatic
tool works, started at Fraserburgh in 1905 and enlarged in
1932, was an appreciation of the potential of a burgh with a
substantial population and good rail communications.

Finally, the Highland situation exhibited a number of
trends which were as controversial then as current developments
are now. The resources of the area suggested a range of
'natural' industries. The distinctive woollen industries of
the Western Isles and Shetland, with their emphasis on domestic
weaving and knitting, continued to survive, promoted in the
former case by the Harris Tweed Association which sought to
ward off foreign imitation through the introduction of a
registered trademark and to preserve the island-based occupation
against competition from mainland yarn producers and finishers
at Brora and Inverness. Then the seaweed industry was revived:
Lochboisdale (Western Isles) was the centre for the collection
of seaweed for the iodine industry, while in Kintyre (Argyll &
Bute) a factory was opened to process seaweed for transparent
wrapping material. The granite industry was found in Argyll at
Furnace and at Bonawe, where new plant was installed in 1937.
Marble from Skye and slate from Ballachulish was worked, and
there was optimism over the prospects for renewed working of
metallic ores in Islay, Skye and Sutherland. Sand and lime were
being worked and a new brickworks opened at Lairg (Sutherland)
in 1937. But against this consolidation of primary industry
there was the prospect of an expansion in tourism, and, still
more controversial, the possibility of large-scale industry
based on hydroelectricity. The aluminium industry was a
reality, with factories at Foyers (Inverness), Kinlochleven
and Fort William (Lochaber), but the Caledonian Power Bill
would allow further works, in Glen Garry and Glen Moriston,
with power from generators at Loch Hourn, Cluanie, Invergarry
and Invermoriston fed to a proposed calcium-carbide factory at
Corpach, near Fort William. Amenity interests defeated the
plan, and the problems of remote rural areas digesting large-
scale industrial developments were thereby contained. But the
debate on the optimum scale and nature of Highland industrialisation continued.

In 1953 C. A. Oakley produced a further review of
Scottish industry, in which lists were included of the major
companies (Fig 6).[36] The few large industries outside the
Central Belt represent the fragments remaining after short
periods of speculative early nineteenth-century diffusion.
Changed circumstances, less attractive for the Outer Regions,
have seen some firms eliminated, while others have countered

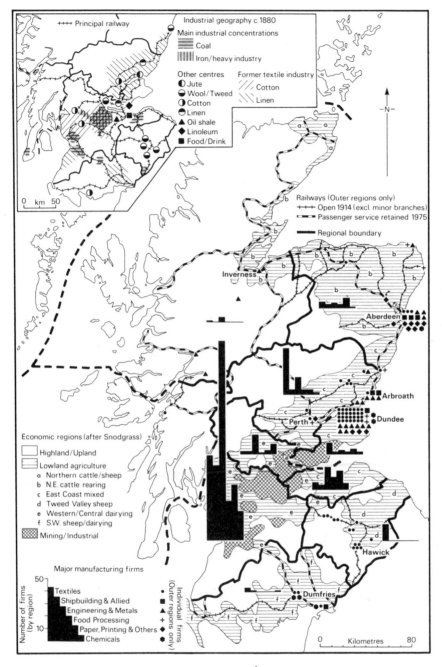

Fig 6 Economic regions before WWII (C.P. Snodgrass — cf note 37)

locational weakness by innovation and specialisation. Although
their contribution has been locally very great, it is evident
that in the Outer Regions as a whole manufacturing has failed
to offer adequate replacement for the losses arising from the
contraction of the primary industries. These primary activities
have an enduring importance and were seen by C. P. Snodgrass
as fundamental in the recognition of economic regions.[37]   Much
thought was being given to the modification of industrial
patterns, reflected in the literature of the period.[38]
Misgivings were being expressed about the unacceptably high
level of concentration of industry in parts of the Central Belt
and an almost total lack of manufacturing in some of the Outer
Regions. Scotland as a whole needed new industries. Indeed
Oakley's 1937 study was in part a propaganda exercise to
publicise the dynamism, after years of depression and emigration,
of Scottish industry. But the geography was also a matter for
consternation.

There was a growing public concern over the fate of the
declining rural periphery. The infrastructure needed rebuilding
to accommodate electricity supply, road modernisation and new
housing. The problems of the Highlands were underlined in a
Scottish Economic Committee publication, issued at a time of
growing public concern, expressed by the call for the formation
of a Highland Development Board in 1936.[39]   A more promising
economic climate helped to create an atmosphere for local
development. The Leverhulme project in Lewis and Harris,
although abandoned, had demonstrated the logic of a comprehensive programme with land reclamation strengthening a system of
farms, with ancillary occupations in fishing and processing.
Areas like Orkney and Kintyre (Argyll & Bute) with better
resources for farming might sustain intensification in
dairying, poultry and horticulture with local processing. On a
rather different scale were the potentials of Inverness,
arising from the quality of its services and labour catchment.
Although its engineering industry had been weakened by railway
amalgamations which eliminated locomotive building and repair,
the Rose Street Foundry and Engineering Company developed a
welding machine which found considerable demand, and Fort
William enjoyed road, rail and sea communications as well as
ample hydroelectricity potential. Prophetically, C.A. Oakley
declared: 'if an industrial centre does develop in the Highlands
during the next twenty years I think it will be at Fort
William'.[40]   The future Highland growth points were already
mapped out!

The Present Industrial Geography

The employment pattern is examined with reference to estimates drawn from each employment exchange for June 1961 and June 1971.[41] Exchanges have been grouped into a total of eighteen employment areas, named after the largest constituent exchange, and the number of sectors used to represent the employment structure has been greatly simplified. The area data is mapped in Fig 7, and the salient features are summarised in Table 1. With 26.3 per cent of the active population (aged over 15) the Outer Regions accounted for 22.5 per cent of insured employees (but 19.0 per cent for manufacturing compared with 71.7 per cent for agriculture, forestry and fishing). There are pronounced regional contrasts, with an agricultural bias in the Highlands and the South (although all regions had a greater share of employment in agriculture than their share of total employment would suggest and, despite a decline in total numbers, all regions have increased their share of jobs in agriculture since 1961). Tayside has a relatively well-developed industry.

Looking at the areas individually it is evident that the primary sector (including mining and quarrying as well as agriculture, forestry and fishing) shows much variation. Whereas values of over 20 per cent are recorded for Blairgowrie, Castle Douglas, Eyemouth and Huntly the proportion falls below 5 per cent in Dundee. There has been a general fall in the numbers employed in this section during the decade by at least 20 per cent, but the rate of decline exceeds 40 per cent in Campbeltown, Dundee, Elgin and Inverness. However, to some extent the losses in the primary sector are balanced by gains in manufacturing. In 1971 only Blairgowrie, Campbeltown, Castle Douglas, Eyemouth and Wick had more jobs in the primary sector than in manufacturing, whereas in 1961 a similar situation obtained in Elgin, Huntly, Inverness and Lerwick as well. Usually, however, the manufacturing shares did not increase enough to compensate for all the losses in primary industry: this happened only in Fraserburgh, Huntly, Lerwick and Wick. The service sectors have also expanded, especially professional and scientific services which have often gained at the expense of the other service category. In every area except Fraserburgh, the two service categories account for more than 40 per cent of the jobs and in some cases the proportion rises above 50 per cent. These latter cases include Blairgowrie (52.2), Elgin (56.0), Aberdeen (56.2) and all the Highland areas where the service sector fluctuates in importance between 55.2 per cent (Lerwick) and 65.0 (Inverness). Some of of these high figures would be anticipated: a high value for

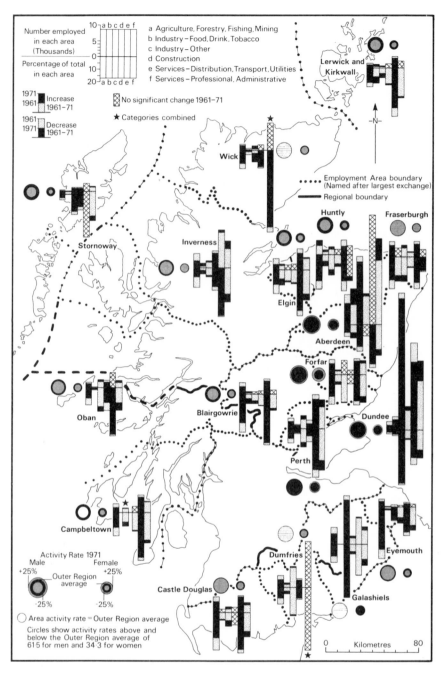

Fig 7 Employment structure 1961 and 1971
(Department of Employment)

Table 1

EMPLOYMENT IN 1961 AND 1971

Number of jobs (000s) and percentage share of Scottish total

Region (1)	Total Employment				Primary Sector				Manufacturing				Active Population	
	1961		1971		1961		1971		1961		1971		1961	1971 (% only)
Highland	82.2	3.8	84.2	3.9	12.8	13.0	7.5	12.8	8.4	1.1	12.0	1.6	5.4	5.5
Grampian	159.5	7.4	157.4	7.4	21.6	22.0	14.5	24.8	38.5	5.1	45.0	6.1	8.5	8.4
Tayside	153.1	7.1	158.1	7.4	14.3	14.6	9.4	16.1	58.0	7.6	56.9	7.7	7.9	7.8
NORTH	394.8	18.3	399.7	18.7	48.7	49.6	31.4	53.7	104.9	13.8	112.9	15.4	21.8	21.7
Borders	41.1	1.9	37.3	1.8	7.6	7.7	4.8	8.2	15.8	2.1	14.6	2.0	2.2	2.0
Dumfries & Galloway	45.0	2.1	43.3	2.0	8.5	8.7	5.8	10.0	9.2	1.2	10.8	1.4	2.6	2.6
SOUTH	86.1	4.0	81.0	3.8	16.1	16.4	10.6	18.2	25.0	3.3	25.4	3.4	4.8	4.6
OUTER REGIONS	480.8	22.3	480.7	22.5	64.8	66.0	42.1	71.7	130.0	17.1	139.3	19.0	26.5	26.3
CENTRAL BELT	1674.2	77.7	1652.7	77.5	33.4	34.0	16.6	28.3	630.2	82.9	597.2	81.0	73.5	73.7
SCOTLAND	2155.0		2133.4		98.2		58.7		760.2		736.5			

1 For Tables 1–4 inclusive the regions are built from employment-exchange areas (see Fig 7). Rothesay exchange is considered part of the Central Belt.

Source: Department of Employment, Edinburgh

Aberdeen, the principal service centre for the North, would be expected, as would a correspondingly low figure for Fraserburgh, which is dependent on Aberdeen for many service functions. Likewise, Inverness has a special service role, augmented by the establishment of branches of the civil service, as does Wick by virtue of the atomic-research station. But the consistently high values for the Highlands are rather surprising; they reflect the weakness of the manufacturing sector and, probably, a degree of overemployment in services for lack of other opportunities, although this sector is bound to employ relatively large numbers in view of the scattered distribution of population.

Not every employment area increased its manufacturing in relation to other sectors. In three areas where textiles were well represented (Dundee, Arbroath, Galashiels and Stornoway) there was a small contraction. Everywhere else there was growth in manufacturing (but only relative, rather than absolute, in Eyemouth) and this was most evident in such less-industrialised rural regions as Blairgowrie, up to 9.0 to 14.6 per cent, and Lerwick, advancing from 10.9 to 19.6. However, Fraserburgh, with a substantial industrial sector, also experienced a rapid growth of manufacturing, from 29.4 to 39.1 per cent and a large number of new jobs were involved in the growth in Inverness from 7.6 to 11.7 per cent. While the improved position in the main towns and cities may be related to their wide range of industries, including sophisticated engineering companies, other areas have developed not so much as a result of broad locational advantages as through the availability of raw material and labour for an expansion of the food-processing industry. Although the rather low wages associated with food, drink and tobacco sector limit the desirability of these branches in the minds of regional economists, their contribution in a number of areas in the North has been numerically strong. In Fraserburgh the estimated number of jobs rose from 2,766 to 3,700 and expansion was felt in all three constituent exchanges Fraserburgh, Peterhead and Turriff. And in Lerwick the increase was from 648 to 1,158. Gains have also been marked in Dumfries, Forfar and Huntly.

More precise figures for individual sectors of manufacturing have been drawn from the census enumeration tables. This source is unsatisfactory in that counties and large burghs are treated rather than the present local-government areas, but many different sectors are covered, allowing broad contrasts and trends to emerge (Fig 8). The distributions will be more closely scrutinised in later chapters, but at this stage it is worth noting the overwhelming importance of Aberdeen and

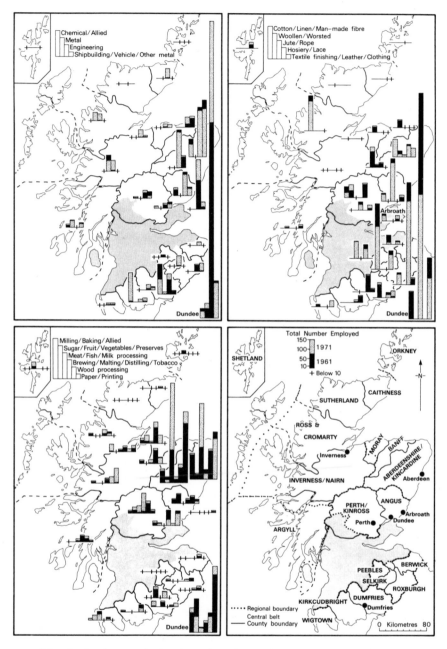

Fig 8 Employment in leading branches of manufacturing
1961 and 1971
(Census of Scotland - Industry and Status Tables - 10% sample)

Table 2

THE FOOD, DRINK AND TOBACCO SECTOR, 1961 AND 1971

Region	Industrial Employment 1971 ('000s)	Employment in Food, Drink & Tobacco, 1971 ('000s)	Percentage Change in Industrial Employment 1961-71	Percentage Change in Employment in FDT 1961-71	FDT employment as a percentage of all industrial employment 1961	FDT employment as a percentage of all industrial employment 1971
Highland	11.99	3.51	42.7	83.4	22.8	29.2
Grampian	45.03	17.92	16.8	62.6	28.6	39.8
Tayside	56.88	7.13	- 2.0	4.3	11.8	12.5
NORTH	113.90	28.55	8.5	44.5	18.8	25.1
Borders	14.57	1.10	- 8.0	43.6	4.5	4.9
Dumfries & Galloway	10.45	2.41	13.6	22.1	21.4	23.0
SOUTH	25.02	2.51	- 0.1	22.8	8.2	10.0
OUTER REGIONS	138.92	31.07	7.2	42.5	16.8	22.3
CENTRAL BELT	597.62	82.81	- 5.2	7.5	12.2	13.9
SCOTLAND	736.54	113.88	- 3.1	15.2	13.0	15.5

Due to a lack of estimates for FDT employment in some Border and Grampian exchange areas, the importance of the sector in these two regions is slightly underrated.

Source: Department of Employment, Edinburgh

Dundee, and the weakness of the Higlands in all sectors except woollen textiles (Ross & Cromarty county) and metals (Inverness county). Beyond this, the major impact of textile sectors in many counties and burghs emerges clearly. The strength of the engineering chemical group in Angus, Dumfries and Fraserburgh Peterhead is relatively impressive, as is the brewing/distilling group in Banff, Perth and Moray & Nairn. From Table 2 it will be seen that the food sector has increased its share in all the regions. Clearly, however, the Grampian region is out-standing, with not only the greatest proportionate increase but with an absolute increase and a final total greater than that of the other three combined. However, the trends in textiles are usually negative, underlining the recession in the industry, and the generally weak economic position in the period immediately before the oil-related activities gathered momentum must be a fundamental consideration in interpreting the changes.

    The employment data may be subjected to other useful analyses. By linking it with census material some measure of activity levels may be gained. Calculation of total registered employees as a percentage of the population above the age of fifteen shows the highest activity levels for Tayside, the lowest for the Highlands (Table 3). These findings apply to both men and women. However, while Blairgowrie is far less active than other areas in Tayside, other regions have their deviations in the relatively high level of activity in Aberdeen, Galashiels and Wick where the rates are above the average for the Outer Regions as a whole (Wick for men only, however). An examination of trends over the decade 1961-71 reveals some overall gain in activity in the Highlands and the Grampian region, and a slight decline in Tayside and the South, the rate for the Outer Regions as a whole being virtually unchanged. However there was a noticeable improvement in female activity, by 7.5 per cent, and a decline in the male sector of 4.9 per cent. These trends were borne out in each region, except that the trends in female activity showed very great increases in the Highlands and the Grampian region as against a decline in the South. Deviations from the Outer Regions' average have increased slightly in respect of male activity in industry since the negative deviation of the Highlands and the positive deviation of Tayside have been reinforced. But the reverse applies for female activity, where the Highlands and Tayside have moved much nearer the average and reduced their previously pronounced negative and positive deviations respectively. Similar trends apply for activity in all branches of employment; the Highlands and Tayside still represent the extremes by

Table 3

ACTIVITY RATES 1961 AND 1971

Region	All employment						Employment in Industry					
	Male		Female		Total		Male		Female		Total	
Highland	52.8	- 7.1	27.7	17.6	39.7	0.7	8.9	37.1	2.7	50.3	5.6	40.2
Grampian	62.7	- 4.9	35.6	14.1	48.4	3.0	18.9	11.9	9.2	23.1	13.8	16.3
Tayside	66.9	- 3.5	39.2	1.2	52.1	- 1.4	25.6	3.7	12.9	- 10.9	18.8	- 2.0
NORTH	61.6	- 4.9	34.9	9.4	47.5	0.6	18.7	10.0	8.9	2.3	13.5	7.1
Borders	61.4	- 7.1	35.3	- 1.7	47.4	- 4.8	22.1	3.8	15.1	- 12.7	18.4	- 4.2
Dumfries & Galloway	60.5	- 2.7	28.6	- 2.4	43.8	- 2.5	15.3	15.0	6.9	25.5	10.9	18.4
SOUTH	60.9	- 4.7	31.7	- 1.9	45.4	- 3.6	18.3	9.0	10.6	- 3.0	14.2	3.6
OUTER REGIONS	61.5	- 4.9	34.3	7.5	47.1	- 0.1	18.6	9.8	9.2	1.6	13.7	7.0
CENTRAL BELT	75.1	- 8.4	42.7	7.0	57.9	- 2.4	30.6	- 6.7	12.3	- 6.1	20.9	- 6.3
SCOTLAND	71.5	- 7.6	40.5	7.1	55.1	- 1.8	27.5	- 3.8	11.5	- 4.2	19.0	- 4.0

Calculated against the total population over fifteen years of age. In each case the 1971 rate and the percentage change since 1961 are given

Source: Department of Employment, Edinburgh and Census of Scotland

considerable margins, the Grampian region has consolidated its positive deviations, whereas the South has slipped further behind. In both cases the movement arises through changes in the female sector.

These comments lead on to a summary of the ratios of male to female jobs in different areas. For all employment there is movement towards 'equality' evident in all regions, with the Highlands showing the greatest change, leaving it only marginally behind the South (Table 4). However for <u>industrial</u> employment alone the Highland situation is far less favourable. Notwithstanding some improvement, there were still in 1971 three times as many jobs for men as for women, compared with the ratio of 1.8 for the Outer Regions as a whole. Despite their retention of the lowest ratios, both Tayside and the South, however, show increases over the decade, due to the difficulties in the textile industry. Of course the regional figures obscure very substantial variations in the different areas and exchanges, as shown in Fig 9. Attention is drawn to the very high industrial ratio for Oban of 5.08, resulting from the bias to heavy industry in Lochaber, compared with the very low ratio of 1.27 for Galashiels. For all employment, Galashiels retains the lowest ratio (1.43), while Wick has the highest at 2.01, followed by Eyemouth at 1.97, and Dumfries at 1.91. Unemployment trends are also shown in Fig 9. The relatively favourable situation in Tayside and the Borders, the seasonal fluctuations in the Highlands, the impact of oil-related employment at Invergordon and the problem of pit closures at Sanquhar are brought out.

Conclusion

The Outer Regions, by their very nature, comprise a broad periphery with little evidence of concentration and congestion. Highly specialised and structured industrial regions could hardly be anticipated in view of the succession of currents to which remoter parts of Scotland have been exposed. The ripples, spreading from successive innovations in West-Central Scotland (fine linen, cotton, iron, heavy engineering) failed to spread far beyond the Central Belt, although the cumulative effect has been to push to the periphery certain of the less-profitable and dynamic industries which could not continue to compete successfully for labour and capital in the centre. The periphery does have its own internal contrasts, reflecting degrees of accessibility to innovation from the centre and variations in other local resources which have attracted large shares of total investment in particular Scottish industries. But the problems of the periphery, in terms of structural imbalance and

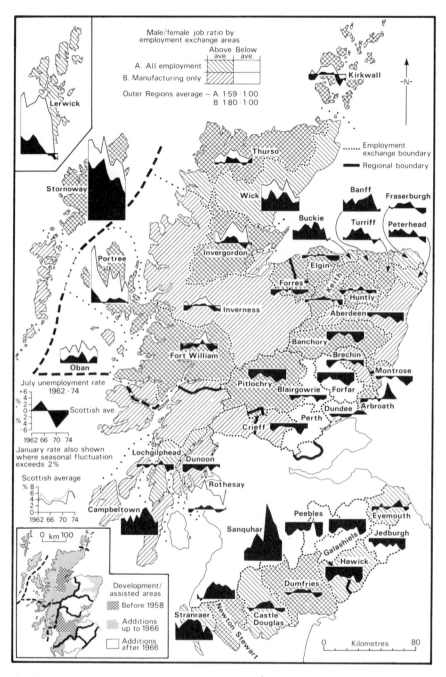

Fig 9 Further aspects of employment (<u>Department of Employment</u>)

persistent unemployment, are general enough to impart a certain
homogeneity, though the extent of the imbalance and the
seriousness of unemployment shows variations within the Outer
Regions greater than the variation between the Central Belt
and the Outer Regions as a whole, especially since the Central
Belt is wrestling with its own problems of reconstruction.
The following chapters are drafted to explore the distinctive
spatial expression of some particular industries and the
broader regional socio-economic question on which industry as
a whole impinges.

Table 4

SEX RATIOS IN EMPLOYMENT 1961 AND 1971

Region	Number of male jobs for each female job			
	Total Employment		Employment in Industry	
	1961	1971	1961	1971
Highland	2.21	1.75	3.32	3.03
Grampian	1.86	1.56	1.95	1.83
Tayside	1.52	1.49	1.45	1.74
NORTH	1.76	1.57	1.72	1.87
Borders	1.58	1.50	1.05	1.26
Dumfries & Galloway	1.91	1.89	2.17	1.97
SOUTH	1.74	1.69	1.36	1.52
OUTER REGIONS	1.77	1.59	1.64	1.80
CENTRAL BELT	1.80	1.56	2.21	2.20
SCOTLAND	1.79	1.56	2.10	2.12

Source: Department of Employment, Edinburgh

2

Textiles: Spread and Specialisation

It would be difficult to find a more traditional industry in
Scotland than that of textile manufacture. Production of
woollen cloth or plaiding was a basic domestic craft providing
for the family, and in some cases generating a surplus for sale
locally or for export. Before the Union, attempts were made to
improve the quality of woollen cloth, but the Scottish industry
succumbed heavily to English competition. However, there were
opportunities for development with other types of cloth during
the eighteenth century. There was considerable optimism over
linen cloth production, an industry which had good prospects
in English markets as well as at home and which, it seemed,
could be sustained throughout Scotland by flax grown locally.
Textiles held out great hopes for the rural areas because of
their potential contribution to the stronger village communities
needed to resettle people displaced from the land, and because
they offered a local market for agricultural produce. The
villages might be the production points and, additionally, they
might market cloth produced domestically in the surrounding
areas. Good water-power resources were a particularly powerful
incentive: at Auchterarder (Perth & Kinross) rather modest
Ruthven Burn 'at all seasons of the year conveys such a
quantity of water it is sufficient to turn the machinery of
any ordinary mill'.[1] And Sanquhar (Nithsdale), with wool cloth,
carpet and stocking industries, was 'an unrivalled situation
where there is plenty of water and descent to drive weighty
machinery', not to mention the nearby coal seams.[2] Great
optimism was placed in the future: the water power of such
places as East Linton, Lauder and Moffat, in the Borders, was
very suitable for woollen industries and Sir John Sinclair
appreciated the potential of textile industries for Highland
development 'if villages were established over the great part
of the Highlands and especially along the sea shores and banks
of the Caledonian and Crinan canals; and if small branches of
our manufactures were thus spread over the country'.[3]

44

From the Statistical Account it is possible to identify
the parishes where the textile industry was important, and the
evidence is summarised in Fig 10. The exercise is fraught with
problems: the tremendous variations in the quality of the
parish reports and their contrasts in detail and approach make
it impossible to gain anything more than a general qualitative
impression. In many parishes it is not clear how far an
integrated industry was being carried on or whether merely
spinning, weaving or finishing was established. Nevertheless,
the generalised data does produce a picture worthy of some
consideration. The paucity of references in the Highlands is a
striking feature. Although local woollen production must have
been widespread, it is clear that commercial activity was very
limited. The greatest activity was in Tayside and to a rather
lesser extent in the Grampian region: a commercial woollen
industry survives despite the popularity of linen and the
beginning of the cotton industry round Perth. In the South,
activity is relatively scattered with woollens well established
in the Borders, linen prominent in Nithsdale and cotton in
Stewartry. Some of the industries were very successful. Deanston
(Perth & Kinross) was later described as a 'handsome little
village' for its factory had 'changed the face of the country
by introducing into it habits of industry and the highest
mechanical genius and dexterity'.[4] The spread of industry was
limited, but all branches of the textile sector are still
present in Scotland, with the Outer Regions well represented.
However, the location pattern has no clear logic, apart from
the relative importance of the Outer Regions which might be
anticipated to follow from the competition exerted by more
sophisticated and profitable industries in the Central Belt.
Within the Outer Regions we are confronted with a relict
industrial pattern with the survival of enterprises which were
once part of a more comprehensive system. The following sections
deal first with the rapid diffusion and subsequent consolidation
of linen and cotton textiles, and second with the conversion of
the widespread domestic woollen industry into a producer of
quality products.

The Boom in Linen and Cotton

    Most prominent on the map is the evidence of the linen
industry. This has been described as 'Scotland's premier
industry in the eighteenth century', playing a leading role in[5]
the transformation of the Scottish economy during this period.
Market prospects for linen were good and the cultivation of
flax fitted in well with an agricultural system which had not
yet experienced the full draught of improvement. Encouragement

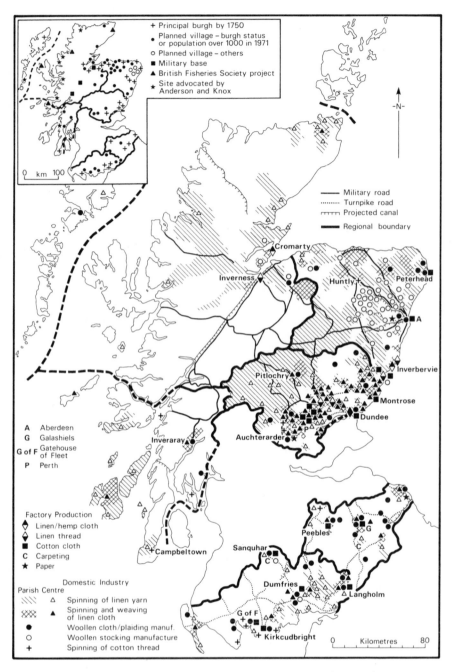

Fig 10 Eighteenth century textiles and (inset)
the planned village (OSA)

was forthcoming from the Board of Trustees for Manufactures set up in 1727 to administer funds for industrial development promised to the Scots under the terms of the Union The money was provided as compensation, related to the embargo on the export of raw wool from Britain, an injunction already in force in England but now applied to Scotland where wool had previously been exported to the continent at higher prices than those obtaining south of the border. Textiles were an obvious target for the Board's efforts. But, as was pointed out in 1735 by Sir Patrick Lindsay, one of its early presidents, the difficulty of developing a high-quality and competitively priced woollen cloth due to inadequate expertise especially in the finishing sector, made it desirable to concentrate the effort on linen because here there was a cost advantage in Scotland's favour. After many years of delay in implementing the scheme for compensation, the Board applied much energy to the daunting task of improving the quality and quantity of linen cloth. Premiums were granted for cultivation and preparation: skilled flax dressers were brought in to teach the best methods, spinning schools were established and subsidies provided for the laying out of bleachfields.[6] But a balance had to be struck between the improvement of the quality of cloth and competitive pricing. Although there was some friction with the Board because of irregularities, there can be no doubt that the Dundee people proved to be most adept at keeping costs down and producing cloth which could find a ready market in the colonies. The manufacture of coarse linen apparently began by chance in Arbroath when a weaver made a web of linen from low-quality yarn. Experiments were made to the point where the business was capable of promotion. The industry spread to Forfar where it induced 'great alterations in the appearance of the place and the manners of its inhabitants', although the trade was said to be a fluctuating one and slack demand 'brings many of the young and unprovident into difficulties'.[7]

The Tayside industry took full advantage of the bounty system applied in 1742 in order to stimulate production for export. In parts of the Grampian region, notably Cullen (Moray), substantial progress was made, with encouragement from Lord Deskford, one of the Board's trustees. Dutch flax was obtained and lint mills and bleachfields provided. Aberdeen merchants were very active in importing flax and distributing it in the rural areas, for local flax cultivation was usually inadequate. But after the rebellion of 1745, strenuous attempts were made to spread the industry through the Highlands. To assist this new drive, the bounty system was dropped in 1753 in favour of a fund of £3,000 to finance a nine-year expansion programme for the region.[8] Manufacturers would organise collection and distribution of materials through intakers based at strategic points. A number of spinning schools were already in existence, at Beauly (Inverness), Campbeltown (Argyll) and Tain (Ross & Cromarty), but stations were now established at Glenmoriston (Inverness), Loch Broom (Ross & Cromarty) and Loch Carron (Skye & Lochalsh) by 1755. But the industry was not successful. Many areas were unsuitable for flax growing and lint therefore had to be imported from Holland at relatively high cost.[9] The transport system was unsatisfactory, leading to delays in distribution and higher production costs: even in Strathavon, in the upland districts of Moray, it was the very high cost of the finished product that made expansion impossible.[10] The attempt by the Forfeited Estates Commissioners to introduce flax raising and spinning to Lewis in the Western Isles was frustrated by the difficulty of finding merchants who could operate a viable business, and in Shetland it was remarked that the fair sex 'could not apply themselves with diligence to the manufacturing process'.[11] There were some local successes: as a result of the distribution of free linseed, beginning in 1770, the proprietor of Holm (Orkney) was successful in stimu- lating flax production and building up a linen-export business. But the returns were evidently insufficient to justify continu- ation of the scheme after his death when the industry collapsed from lack of encouragement. There was little progress beyond the Highland margins, and even here most of the effort was expended in spinning imported flax 'done by commission for southern districts where weaving takes place'.[12] It is curious that linen was never very important in the South, where it was simply a domestic craft, with significant flax cultivation only in Lower Annandale, around Lochmaben, and at Stranraer. It had evidently succumbed to competition from the Tayside industry by the 1820s.

The application of spinning machinery dates from experiments at Brigton (Angus) and Inverbervie (Kincardine and Deeside) in the 1780s, but satisfactory equipment for spinning fine thread was only developed in the 1820s. In the following decades hand spinning declined rapidly. There was little opportunity at Deskford (Moray) in the 1840s, for when flax was available there was 'the greatest possible scramble among the old women to get a share of it'.[13] Domestic work in weaving cloth was also yielding poorer returns. Grave social problems arose from the oversupply of labour (complicated by Irish immigration) which depressed wages even beyond the point at which it would have been competitive to introduce machinery, but government intervention seemed inappropriate in view of the highly

informal organisation of the domestic industry and the difficulty in transferring labour to other occupations.[14] At Alyth
(Angus), many weavers would have been in a state of 'melancholy
destitution if they had not an opportunity of eking out their
scanty means by assisting in the harvest work on the neighbouring
farms'.[15] But the rural problems in the Grampian region were
alleviated by the considerable opportunities in agriculture and
fishing, and disappearances of the linen industry from the
planned villages (as well as the eclipse of the hemp industry
in Cromarty and Inverness) was balanced by the expansion of the
new growth industries. Tayside was more successful in developing
a factory industry. Arbroath 'obtained the best machinery that
was known in the trade and by devoting great care to the
manufacture succeeded in producing a better quality of goods',
but it was above all in the Dundee area that the industry
expanded through 'the perseverance of the manufacturers in
adopting and improving machinery for superseding hand labour,[16]
cheapening production and improving the quality of the work'.
Based in a major port, Dundee merchants had wide marketing
experience and capital invested in the industry spread to
locations throughout the region. Evidently, Perth had initially
played an important role in the growth of the Strathmore
industry with a major expansion of bleachfields from 1774
when the Huntingtower field was laid out, and some diffusion
of capital through the Sandeman business, supplementing wealth
derived locally through corn milling.[17] However, the subsequent
development of bleaching by Sandeman's on the Dighty Burn near
Dundee is considered to mark a change towards a greater
appreciation of Dundee's potential for organising the region's
industry, stemming from its better port facilities and improved
accessibility with the inland towns through the turnpikes, and
later the railways. Towns such as Brechin, Forfar and Kerriemuir
tended to be centres of weaving dependent on yarn produced in
Dundee, but Blairgowrie had its own water-powered spinning
capacity, still at work in 1967. At the same time Perth's
facilities were employed in the context of a reduced hinterland
for the cotton industry, and new links developed with Glasgow
manufacturers.

     The transition period from linen to jute began in Dundee
with experiments carried out in 1832 as part of an attempt
to develop new cheap bagging materials. Competition from the
cotton industry forced linen producers to concentrate on
coarser cloth, using such low-grade materials as tow (short
coarse flax fibres) and codilla (waste material removed from
flax during the scutching process), for which spinning machinery
was developed in the 1820s. It was found that the jute fibres
could be softened with whale oil and used for a tough, porous

and repairable fabric first accepted for bagging by the export trade in 1838. Production was fully mechanised during the 1850s when there was a decisive shift towards jute because of the interruption of flax supplies through the Crimean War. Easily dyed in bright colours, jute was mixed with flax for the production of lower-quality goods, and in the 1870s flax was completely superseded except for canvas and tarpaulin sheeting when the cotton famine improved opportunities for jute and brought the culmination to Dundee's Victorian prosperity.[18] Dundee was able to attract the jute clippers all the way to the Tay (the first shipments were received via London), and the trade helped to further the expansion of the port at a time when the coasting trade was in decline. City trends were followed by the inland towns and by Inverbervie where flax, tow and, later, jute was worked. The 'Indian summer' enjoyed by the industry immediately before and during World War I was to complicate the problem of diversification, which had to be faced when Asian competition became serious. Finer-quality products and a higher level of technical inventiveness retained a share of the industry for stronger firms which combined the spinning, weaving and ancillary processes and replaced the individualism of the small business. The movement has been strengthened since World War II by the British Jute Trade Research Association, set up with premises in Dundee in 1946. High-quality jute yarn has special uses in power cables and pipe joints, but the main outlet is backing yarn for Axminster and Wilton carpets.

More significant, however, is the development of a multifibre industry making particular use of polypropylene. Plastic film split into tapes may be woven into industrial fabric, and the same material is used to supplement jute for tufted carpet backing. In the packaging field the competition of the paper-sack manufacturers is now being countered by the use of polypropylene transparent materials. Then viscose and nylon are used by Jute Industries for the production of 'Thistlecord'. Use of the new fibres once again extends to the inland towns and to Inverbervie, and supplements the continued output of coarse and linen products such as canvas, sailcloth and webbing.

By the end of the eighteenth century, cotton was capturing the imagination, and once again there was an initial boom which pushed the industry into the peripheral areas.[19] The rapid expansion of the linen industry led not only to rising imports of flax, the cost of which remained high, for the bottleneck caused by a shortage of spinners was grave enough to encourage

technical change. Ironically, 'the first beneficiary was not
linen but the usurper, cotton'.[20] The cotton industry was
concentrated in Glasgow at first, an area noted for its fine
cloth production and for the resourcefulness of its merchants,
who were in close touch with developments on the continent.
During the 1770s and 1780s there were several developments in
Lanarkshire and Renfrewshire as well as Rothesay (Argyll & Bute).
This area remained the core of the industry, eventually to be
destroyed by competition from Lancashire and from other
industries in the Clyde area which competed for capital and
labour. But more important, during the water-power era, the
industrialists reached out to the best power sites. The mills
of Deanston and Stanley in Perth & Kinross are prime examples
of large water-powered spinning units with satellite villages
of weavers, such as Battleby.[21] Speculators believed that
Pitcairn Green might ultimately rival Manchester, although in
contrast to the hamlet of New Leeds (Banff & Buchan) this
optimism does not appear to have been written into the name of
the settlement. However, despite considerable contraction,
Stanley still sews cotton tape while Deanston produces sheets
and towelling with cotton drawn from Lancashire. Also cotton
furnishing fabrics are produced at Perth.

Another remarkable story in the industrial growth of the
Outer Regions at the time of the improving movement is the
cotton industry's successful implantation in Dumfries and
Galloway. While William Craik of Arbigland concentrated on the
new husbandry, Sir William Douglas and James Murray threw
their weight behind the region's industrial potential. From
the late 1780s, Douglas lavished the proceeds of his business
career on his estate with the twin settlements of Castle
Douglas and Newton Douglas (later Newton Stewart) winning a
complex of industries including cotton spinning, carpet manufacture, tanning, brewing and handloom weaving. The large
cotton mill on the Cree at Newton Douglas was complemented by
a smaller hand-spinning mill in Castle Douglas where water
power was lacking. Both mills survived until the trade
depression shortly after the founder's death, when, it has been
argued by I. L. Donnachie, they succumbed for the lack of good
management.[22] James Murray was associated with the cotton
industry in Gatehouse of Fleet where water power was provided
through a system of lades emanating from Loch Whinyeon four
miles away and serving groups of factories in the centre of
the village and on its eastern edge. Among the centre group
was the Birtwhistle cotton mill erected by outside industrialists attracted to the town by its favourable situation. As well
as a location on the turnpike road, Gatehouse had its harbour,
Port Macadam, and a canal which improved access to it. Also

important were the generous leasing arrangements. The four
cotton mills at work at Gatehouse 'roused a passion for cotton
manufacture through this whole country'.[23] Annan and Langholm
also attracted the industry. Some capacity survived until mid-
century, but the smaller units were in trouble at the end of
the Napoleonic Wars. Mills at Langholm and Newton Douglas
turned to woollens, with tweed growing in popularity, and other
premises were adapted to a variety of other purposes, including
corn milling and warehousing.

The connections enjoyed by people in this area with the West
Central Scotland, Lancashire and Ulster no doubt assisted in
attracting interest. Remoter areas tried to exploit their local
site advantages at the height of the boom. The most remarkable
case is that of Spinningdale in the Sutherland parish of Creich.
Young people were taking seasonal work in the South. 'There
they got high wages, and returned in winter to their parents
or relations, somewhat in the style of gentlemen, and were a
burden on their friends the whole winter until they set out
again in spring.'[24] To afford permanent employment at home,
George Dempster purchased an estate in 1786 and set about
exploiting the water power and sea access afforded at the
Spinningdale site. George MacIntosh and David Dale, with close
connections with the Glasgow cotton industry, subscribed capital
and 'made some progress in erecting a manufacture of spinning
cotton by jennies and weaving their yarn', apparently under
the guidance of instructors sent from Glasgow. A village was
being lotted out close to the mill, and another settlement was
under construction further east where larger vessels could be
accommodated and a warehouse built. 'By these means constant
employment will be found for people of all ages and sexes, and
a considerable market opened for the productions of the
country.'[25] A linen industry was to be established alongside,
and spinning and weaving would be dispersed across the countryside as an ancillary to the cultivation of smallholdings. But
the company seems to have been under-capitalised: the mill was
ready in 1794 but had exhausted the company's resources. Work
continued for some years on borrowed money until 1804 when the
remaining partners put the mill up for sale. It was gutted by
fire two years later.

Both the linen-jute and cotton industries show a remarkable
diffusion phase, with initial growth in the Central Belt
followed by widespread promotion in the Outer Regions. Spread
did not extend significantly into the Highlands, and the
incomplete expansion phase was followed by contraction and
consolidation which leaves only Tayside with a stake in both

industries (although especially in jute and heavy linen).
Such groupings are very significant in the Scottish context
because competition from heavy industries has tended to reduce
the scope for textiles within the Central Belt. Despite this
the linoleum industry, with use of jute as a backing material
developed on the edge of the Fife coalfield at Kirkcaldy.
Tayside (the least peripheral of the Outer Regions), was able
to advance industrially in the context of changing power and
transport technology. By contrast, at Aberdeen, where there
was an early expansion of textiles similarly related to
established mercantile activity, the age of steam reduced the
city's ability to compete. The Grandholm mill was erected on
the lower Don around 1790 when water-powered spinning was first
introduced to the region, but the owners, Lees Masson failed
during the disastrous period 1848-54 after which only two of
the city's major textile firms survived. Although a slump in
business was the immediate cause, failure was 'the inevitable
outcome of Aberdeen's handicaps in the new industrial era'
which would have to be overcome by further improvements in
quality and specialisation.[26] Such has been the response by
Messrs Richards, with premises at the Broadford Mill and also
at Garthdee, on the former bleachfields, devoted to certain
heavy-linen products. Jute industries, however, were withdrawn
before World War I. Aberdeen retains a mixed textile industry
(heavy linen, hosiery, wollens) which provided 2.6 thousand
jobs in 1971, but this is small compared with Dundee's 12.3
thousand (18.9 in 1961) which amounts to the greatest concentration of textile employment in the Outer Regions, with rather
more jobs than the whole of the Borders (10.5).

The Borders Tweed Industry[27]

The Border abbeys were important wool producers in the
Middle Ages, and by the end of the thirteenth century Melrose
Abbey (founded by David I in 1136) was exporting wool on a
scale similar to the great Cistercian foundations in Yorkshire.
But not until the seventeenth century was there any sustained
effort to improve home production of woollen cloth and reduce
dependence on foreign sources for the better-quality goods.
Flemish weavers settled near Edinburgh in 1601, and government
encouragement for the industry led to mill projects at Ayr,
Edinburgh (Bonnington) and Haddington. These ventures were
under-capitalised and found both skilled labour and fine-
quality wool difficult to come by. However, the New Mills
venture at Haddington persisted and was able to benefit from
the prohibition imposed in Scotland against English cloth in
1681. Although the material was rather poor in both quality and

quantity, encouraging merchants to circumvent the embargo and
import better and cheaper cloth from England, the mill was able
to survive until the Treaty of Union, when all barriers to
trade with England were removed.[28]

Despite the eighteenth century preoccuption first with
linen and later with cotton, it seems that several wool mills
were built. Information from the travel reports of David Loch
in the 1770s, examined by J. G. Martindale, suggests that there
was some clustering of activity in the Edinburgh and Galashiels
areas, in addition to the smaller industries: Perth, Elgin,
Inverness and Peterhead in the North are mentioned along with
Ayr, Kilmarnock and Moffat.[29] No doubt there was a considerable
element in chance in the selection process, but Aberdeen also
shared in the seventeenth-century expansion of the industry.
Cloth was produced at the House of Correction in the 1630s, but
more substantial results followed the settlement of Flemish
weavers at Gilcomston after 1680 because they made a valuable
technical contribution and stimulated exports of plaiding and
fine-knitted worsted stockings. There was a rapid growth of
the latter during the eighteenth century, and by the 1770s
some twenty mercantile houses were organising supplies of wool
to a handicraft industry widely practised in the rural areas
as an ancillary to agriculture. Rather heavy dependence on
foreign markets, reached from Aberdeen, restricted the spread
of the industry: after a rapid growth in popularity, which
extended interest to large parts of the North, activity became
consolidated in a more localised area close to the port.[30]
This production area was, however, 'invaded' by the linen
industry and further restricted to parishes unsuitable for
local flax cultivation. The New Statistical Account only
mentions knitting in the areas of Banchory, Alford, Kennethmont,
Fyvie and Turriff, where a number of the older folk were
knitting gloves and socks for very slim returns to supplement
the 'parish money'. Except in the case of Birse, near Banchory,
where local wool was used, the women dealt with agents based
in Aberdeen and Huntly. There was also some outworking for
hosiery factories in the Grampian region which continued the
tradition, in a few cases, until World War I.

For woollen cloth production the eighteenth century,
developments in the Borders mark an early stage in the growth
of a highly successful Scottish industry, and one which merits
a detailed examination.[31] There was an ample wool supply
locally which led several landlords in Roxburgh, notably
Archibald Douglas of Cavers, to campaign for assistance in the
development of local industry to make use of it. The wool was

rather coarse and also tarred, but there proved to be a demand for it in England, where goods were produced for the Atlantic market. The Borders were well placed to integrate with the English industry and profit from the diffusion of spinning skills. The Board of Trustees assisted with instruction, and skilled wool staplers were introduced to several Border towns in 1728: Galashiels, Hawick, Jedburgh, Lauder and Peebles. The commercial links with England were also developed through Border women being employed as outworkers for southern manufacturers, but until agriculture was fully 'improved' labour was in short supply. However, during the last two decades of the century misgivings over the linen industry allowed more attention to be focussed on the woollen trade in Scotland, and the Borders attracted some of the interest at a time when the industry in Central Scotland was losing ground to new trades. With greater local entrepreneurship and a wider range of manufacturing skills, a competitive autonomous industry might arise. There was a considerable domestic production of plaiding throughout the hill country, but renewed encouragement found a particularly strong response in Galashiels. The local 'Gala Tweed' was promoted by a manufacturers' corporation founded in 1777 and improved carding, spinning and finishing systems incorporated in water-powered mills erected in Galashiels in 1791. The industry was still largely a domestic one, although the organisation was fairly sophisticated.[32] Grants made by the Board of Trustees to the Galashiels woollen manufacturers were not infrequently motivated by the need for employees to travel to England and get information and experience of new machinery.

Momentum built up past the turn of the century. Carding and spinning machinery became more general and the factory industry developed, drawing in a growing labour force released from the land by a belated agricultural reorganisation. Moreover, the official encouragement to improve quality and increase the range of local products found a ready response from leading figures in the community who, because of limited agricultural resources and the absence of more profitable industries, were prepared to throw their whole commercial weight behind it. The coarse cloth had some success in competition with Yorkshire, but the factor of a large female labour supply complementing male jobs in heavy industry, and working thereby to supply a large local demand for lower-quality products, was absent from the Border scene. The breakthrough occurred after the end of the Napoleonic wars, by which time several modern mills had been built. Despite some contraction, the core of the industry survived because of the promotion of new tweed designs, and the use of increasing

quantities of imported wool first appreciated late in the
seventeenth century.[33] The basic shepherd's check was modified
by the use of finer wools, and the blending-in of suitable
colours: it proved a very suitable and flexible base for
adaptation at a time when there was a rising demand for heavy
cloth from the upper-class travellers, and a growing independence from French fashions which had previously inhibited
British inventiveness. The tweeds based on machine spinning,
and on power looms first used successfully in Galashiels,
proved highly popular and the Borders became the leading
diffusion centre. Briefly, therefore, to quote from the
argument developed at length by C. Gulvin, the Border industry
was favoured by fashion at a critical moment when the region's
capacity for innovation was being stretched by the competition
from Yorkshire in the market for coarse cloth, yet while there
was still a great enough committment to the woollen industry to
take full advantage of new opportunities.[34] Travellers wanted
a substantial and fashionable cloth and Sir Walter Scott who,
providentially, lived near to Galashiels and was a frequent
visitor to London, helped to nourish the romantic appeal of
Scotland and Scottish products. The Borders gradually strengthened the association with the high-class trade, and the coarse
'blues' and 'greys', which predominated in the 1820s, were
rapidly eclipsed after 1830.

Such considerations help to explain the persistence of a
strong woollen textile industry in the Border counties. But an
equally fascinating geographical theme is the selection process
operating among the Border towns. Galashiels was the principal
centre of the Tweed industry, and its advantages lay in the
water and power resources of the Ettrick, which not only has a
substantial flow but a relatively steep fall permitting a
cluster of mills.[35] And whereas landed interests in other
burghs (Jedburgh, Selkirk and Hawick) were reluctant to grant
feus in case industrial development should compromise their
property or status, the atmosphere in Galashiels was favourable
to growth. Other sites were used once the labour and power
capacity of Galashiels was approaching exhaustion. Henry
Ballantyne moved out to the Gala Valley and established the
textile village of Walkerburn in 1847. There was plenty of
space, although the water supply was less regular and the
gradient much more gentle and less conducive to a large concentration of mills. So when Ballantyne's sons were set up in
business, mill sites were found at Innerleithan and Peebles,
although the 1850s did bring one further mill to Walkerburn,
a spinning factory for Ballantyne's weaving sheds. In his
account of Scottish industrial and social history, J. MacKinnon

claims that the Galashiels weavers were 'an independent set of
men, working only from Tuesday or Wednesday to Saturday and
drinking or fishing on Monday', suggesting that part of the
motive for pioneering new sites arose from the stimulus to
build an independent industrial community.[36] Selkirk was
another location favoured by the explosion of the industry in
Galashiels and was developed quite late, in the 1890s according
to MacKinnon. The mills, usually taking over cornmill sites,
'proved every bit as successful as those in Galashiels' and
proved better able to withstand the depression of the 1930s.
However, Jedbrugh does not seem to have been seriously considered
as a secondary location for the industry, possibly because of
the rather indirect rail communications of the time. Melrose
was avoided because of the flood risks on the riverside sites,
and at Kelso the lack of adequate water and the strong connection here with the agricultural sector made it difficult for
the woollen industry to develop. So with the disappearance of
the coarse woollen trade in the 1830s the diffusion wave
petered out in this part of the Borders.

     But there was some expansion in Dumfries & Galloway.
Water power was not substantial, but steam-powered looms were
brought in by enterprising Dumfries wool masters to Troqueer
Mill in 1866 and Rosefield in 1885. Tweed making was forced out
of Dumfries by 1930 although at Langholm, where mills opened in
1866 and 1878, the industry still survives. Sanquhar acquired
a tweed industry in 1876, using premises previously occupied
by a carpet industry, an eighteenth-century innovation but one
which had succumbed to competition from the highly mechanised
industries of Glasgow and Kilmarnock. Elsewhere in the region
the woollen industry was of only very slight importance.
Certain waulkmills, which had once fulled domestically woven
cloth, were modernised to accommodate water-powered spinning
and the weaving of blankets and plaiding, notably the Waulkmill
on the Bladnoch at Wigtown and Bar Mill at Mochrum, but only
the Cumlodan mill at Old Minnigaff survived beyond World War I.
Here the situation is similar to that in the Grampian region
where the large mills in a few leading woollen towns such as
Elgin (1791) and Keith (1805) were once complemented by smaller
rural enterprises, each with its own evolving relationship with
the domestic sector. The Grampian industry is based principally
in Aberdeen, for John Crombie helped to establish a mill at
Cothal, Dyce (c. 1800), where Border tweed was copied in the
1830s. In 1859 the firm converted the Grandholm linen mill
into a successful woollen business, specialising eventually
in overcoating.[37] The Kirkburn Mills in Peterhead, founded in
1818, now specialise in suitings. Owned by the same firm is

the old country woolcarding mill at Quartalehouse, near
Stuartfield, which began tweedmaking in 1836 and can still be
partially operated by water power.

This discussion leaves aside the remarkable record of
Hawick as a centre of the hosiery industry, a specialisation
which springs from the introduction of the frame knitting to
Hawick by Baillie John Hardie in 1771.[38] He may well have been
impressed by Aberdeen's success and saw the knitting frame as
a means by which Hawick might offer competition. The innovation
was appreciated and although hosiery coexisted with the
traditional plaiding industry for some decades, the town's
reputation for lambs' wool hose, developed by machine knitting
in the 1820s and 1830s, enabled the specialisation to become
virtually complete. The railway link with Edinburgh (1847)
stimulated expansion which continued to 1890, with yarn drawn
from mills both in the Borders and elsewhere. Growth was
particularly brisk in the 1870s and 1880s when new mills were
built and the hand frame finally abandoned. Hawick's early
inclination to hosiery rather than tweed has been related to
the hard water of both the Teviot and the Slitrig, the latter
being a tributary of the Teviot around which the core of the
town and the earliest mills gathered. But the difference in
hardness, compared with the Tweed or Gala, is too slight for
this to contribute significantly to the explanation. Local
entrepreneurs would naturally incline to a distinctive product
once the Galashiels area had committed itself to tweed.
Attempts by proprietors to extend industry to their estates by
building planned villages – the Duke of Buccleuch at Newcastleton
and Sir William Maxwell at Springfield – were unsuccessful, but
an important outpost of the industry took root in Dumfries in
the 1840s: mechanisation came late but one major firm emerged
from late nineteenth-century amalgamations and is still
operating. Aberdeen is another outlying centre with nineteenth-
century origins. Firms also operate in Huntly and Peterhead.

The Border industry prospered through the nineteenth
century. Having taken the lead in fashion, with a flair for
colourful patterns, the manufacturer-designer was careful to
maintain his position, one which drew emulation from Yorkshire
and continental manufacturers, since it was only by retaining
control of the top slice of the market that the industry could
survive. The small-scale business structure of the industry,
and one where each firm had its own tweed speciality, suited
the industry during the prosperous years. Specialisation went
to the point of discouraging vertical integration of spinning
and weaving sections. Weaving shops only appeared in Galashiels

spinning mills in 1828, marking a trend towards factory ownership even of hand-operated looms; but power looms were immediately
integrated into the spinning firms. However, in the late
nineteenth century, because of the special qualities required
of the yarn and the importance of good design, and at a time
when Yorkshire was offering stiff competition in the quality
sector, it became usual to separate the two sections from the
business point of view. The relatively small scale of operation
could be interpreted through the heavy reliance on water power
in mid-century. This situation must obviously be linked with
the distance from coalfields, so it is hardly surprising that
the large coal depot opened in Galashiels in 1932 supplied few
customers initially. Yet even when the cost of coal had come
down because of the completion of the railway, there was still
a tendency to increase the installed water power in the Borders
(excluding Berwickshire), from 924hp in 1861 to 1,179hp in
1871, although steam power did make much faster progress at
that time (503 to 2054hp) after the installation of the first
steam engine in Galashiels in 1853. As power weaving became
universal, and the frustrations of low river-water levels
unacceptable, steam slowly became the rule.

The prosperous years of the 1860s and 1870s, when there
were high profits to be ploughed into more ostentatious living
for the mill owners, gave way to a more competitive period at
the end of the century. This introduced labour problems.
Although there were few competing industries and insufficient
contact with other parts of Scotland to encourage migration,
the failure for real incomes to rise and for employment to
increase helped to stimulate a migration tradition which
threatened to deplete the labour market. The labour force had
never been prolific, and this must have been a stimulus for the
industry to 'spread', but the maintenance of high wages to
sustain good work standards, a high priority in the industry,
was now being compromised. Furthermore, under conditions of
greater commercial stress, the lack of coordination in the
industry proved to be a weakness. Despite the existence of
organisations such as the Galashiels Manufacturers' Corporation,
it could not marshall any unanimity over major issues of
policy such as the development of lighter and smoother cloth.
Eventually the recession of the 1890s brought out the 'Scottish
worsted' which was very suitable for town wear, and some
lightening was also achieved by reducing the firmness of
traditional cloth. For the very demanding ladies' trade, light
cloths became popular in the 1920s and 1930s and gained a
measure of recognition from the Paris fashion houses. However,
the small family company structure has proved incapable of

finding the financial resources to assimilate new machinery. Rationalisation of the industry, combined with the loss of control to outside capital, have been features of the industry in recent times. And while this has brought about some much-needed modernisation, it also creates instability, since the present companies have no firm commitment to the Borders and could transfer capacity to other locations if labour and other operating problems became too difficult.[39] Commuting has increased, and branch factories have been opened in small towns where female labour is available (for example, Coldstream, Eyemouth, Greenlaw and Jedburgh).

Tweed and Knitwear in the Highlands

The expansion of production since World War II has been marked by the appearance of new industries in the Highlands. In addition to the long-established tweed industry in Inverness, a mill was opened in Oban, while small units of production in the rural areas, pioneered by Highland Home Industries, have recently multiplied with the establishment of Hebridean Knitwear at Bayhead (North Uist) and Gott Bay (Tiree). Skye Crotal Knitwear, with premises in Sleat, may even be able to offer employment to outworkers producing jerseys on hand flat machines. Growth in the Highlands is simulated by the Highlands and Islands Development Board's (HIDB) financial incentives, but small pockets of suitable labour in locations which offer an appropriate image for craft products constitute the basic resources. And it should not be overlooked that the traditional skills have been kept alive in the islands especially, and these are now being deployed through cooperatives or by individual promotion. In two areas, however, Shetland and the Western Isles, the ancillary industry was widespread enough to offer a production potential, appreciated in the last century when community leaders were anxious to find support for local industries. Both industries have achieved a measure of coherence, and, notwithstanding the reintroduction of textiles throughout the region in recent years, offers the most impressive examples of growth combined with the craft image.

The Western Isles were in a particularly vulnerable position, with a poor physical base for subsistence. Fishing never proved an entirely satisfactory ancillary, although it occupied some menfolk in each community, but the widespread practice of home spinning and weaving suggested that the production potential could be considerable – certainly greater than on the mainland where the crofting population was smaller, more dispersed and not so committed to the traditional skills.

60

It appears that in 1844 the Earl of Dunmore persuaded some weavers in Harris to copy the Moray check, and the tweed was so successful that the design was adopted for use by the family and the laird's retainers. Promotion further afield came through Lady Dunmore's introduction of the tweed among friends, and by an Edinburgh businesswoman who visited Harris in 1857 and for some thirty years after managed to market the surplus production of the Harris women. By this time other lairds, including Lady Cathcart in Uist, the Duchess of Sutherland and Lady Seaforth, were joining in the act, anxious to alleviate the economic stress arising from the falling agricultural prices. Fortunately, the Congested Districts Board were prepared to dispense some of their resources on payment of instructors and the purchase of looms and dye boilers. And to maintain the quality of the local wool, which was apparently being destroyed by the practice of despatch to mainland mills for carding and spinning, carding mills were built at Tarbert (Harris) and Stornoway at the turn of the century. In 1906 a combined carding and spinning mill was opened in Stornoway. Meanwhile, the heavier fly-shuttle loom was gaining popularity, especially in Lewis, and this made weaving more of a male occupation; and the craft status of the product was protected by a certification trademark in 1910, granted to a newly formed Harris Tweed Association. It seemed, as the Congested Districts Board reported in 1905, that 'if the industry continues to be carefully fostered and supervised it has a future of great possibilities and will prove to be a useful source of revenue and support to the Western Isles'.[40]

The early twentieth-century growth of the industry was most pronounced in Lewis, and it was here where the Hattersley looms, introduced by Lord Leverhulme in the 1920s, proved most popular. Rural weaving in small croft workshops was integrated with spinning, dyeing and finishing operations in Stornoway mills. In this way 'a skilful balance was struck between a true domestic craft product, selling in limited quantities at a high price, and a mass-produced article; the resulting expansion of production has been the economic salvation of the island of Lewis'.[41] But the formula whereby Harris Tweed is made from Scottish wool (local wool is unsuitable and is therefore sent away for use in the carpet industry), spun, dyed and finished in the Outer Hebrides and handwoven on the crofts, has been difficult to apply and maintain. Only in 1934 was the Harris Tweed Association able to combine the interests of the producers of both handmade and mill-based cloth and apply effective quality controls. To ensure a clear division between the mill and croft sectors, a number of weavers were transferred

from factory to croft. Even so, some users of the traditional
'Harris' methods (domestic spinning and weaving and the use of
natural dyes) continue to organise their own work independently.
Then the Harris Tweed label was adopted by mainland mills for
cloth handwoven but not otherwise manufactured in the Hebrides,
and although this production process continues it was only by
recourse to protracted legal action in 1963 that the use of the
'Harris Tweed' label was denied to this spurious cloth. Now the
demand for a greater output and high financial returns is
causing some crofter-weavers to apply electric motors to their
looms in defiance of the ruling that there should be manual
operation. More significant, however, is the development of a
new loom to weave double-width cloth demanded by many buyers.
While this will cater for the growth of production desired, it
is evident that electric power will be needed and that the
equipment will be too expensive for private ownership to be
possible. Not only is there a risk that the tradition of hand
weaving will be compromised, but the need for the most intensive
use of the new looms in central workshops will break the close
connection with the croft, reducing the crofter's independence
and compromising the validity of the 'Orb' stamp. There has
therefore been a heavy vote against these proposed changes.
These developments occur at a time of controversy about over-
manning in both the mill and croft ends of the organisation,
complicated by growing competition for labour due to the oil-
related industry in Stornoway. With the new industry as a
catalyst of change, it is certain that the Harris Tweed industry
will have to be restructured, but it remains to be seen how far
centralisation can be resisted in the interest of retaining a
craft industry and the social fabric of the townships.

Scarcely less valuable than the island's lucrative fishing
and fish-processing industry, Shetland knitwear shows certain
parallels with Harris Tweed. The distinction of the product
lies first in the 'Fair Isle' patterns, thought to have
originated in Central Asia and later introduced by the Moors
to Spain and diffused by traders to northern Europe. But
another important characteristic of the Shetland product is the
use of soft wool obtained from the Shetland sheep. Handknitting
may be regarded as a traditional ancillary activity. Initially,
in the eighteenth century, the local wool was being used for
stockings of very good quality. It appears that inferior
methods became all too common, and the poorest products hardly
yielded the value of the wool. The Commissioners of Supply
attempted to improve quality by a system of stamping goods
which met a rigorous specification, but more effective was the

informal promotion of quality Shetland products when an Oxford
hosiery dealer introduced Shetland products to London in 1839.
Demand was considerable by the mid-1840s and some specialisation
was induced: 'lacework' shawls in Unst, fancy gloves at
Whiteness and Weisdale, stockings at Nesting and underclothing
at Northmaven. During the present century, however, most demand
has been for the pullover or sweater bearing the Fair Isle
pattern, although the very expensive Unst shawls survived
through the interwar period. Natural dyes, produced from
flowers and lichens, were still in use in Fair Isle in the
1930s, but chemical dyes were used in the rest of Shetland
where the same patterns were assimilated. Tweed is manufactured
in Shetland and, as in the Western Isles, it is a male occupation combining croft-based and power-assisted Hattersley looms
with factory finishing. Total production is very small and
shortage of labour makes any significant expansion unlikely.

As with Harris Tweed, the challenge has been one of
meeting an increasing demand, especially since World War II, in
such a way as to maintain the industry as a craft. The industry
is organised by 28 firms of which twelve (including 3 of the 7
large units) are based in Lerwick. Although some of these firms
include workshops employing a regular labour force, they are
all dependent on outworkers, the numbers varying from around
30 in the small firms to over 200 in the largest units. The
outworkers operate in their own homes, receiving yarn from the
firm and knitting or finishing to set requirements and patterns.
The system yields a valuable ancillary income without any
travelling to work (and in good times the worker can 'shop
around'), while the company benefits by access to labour which
would not be available under a less-formal system and an easy
means of adaptation to fluctuating trade conditions: more of
the risks of fluctuating demand can be placed on the workers
than would be possible under the factory system. The closure
in 1973 of the Urafirth and Yell factories of the Shetland
Knitters Association, and the installation of equipment in the
homes of former employees, suggests the system may well grow
in importance. The outworkers are widely dispersed throughout
the islands, and it is not thought that there are any significant pockets of population without their quota of knitters.
Hence the ancillary income, which makes a valuable contribution
to the vitality of rural life, is evenly spread through the
islands, in contrast to fishing and fish processing where only
certain communities benefit. Indeed the skilled labour supply
(some 350 full-time employees and 3,000 outworkers, of which
2,000 work quite regularly) seems to be virtually exhausted,
but hopefully instruction at schools in the island may help to

maintain if not increase interest in future.[42]

But two other significant issues may be raised, dealing with local coordination and foreign imitation. Although hand processing of the wool ceased by World War II, the methods of knitting the yarn supplied by mainland mills varies from hand-knitting, now comparatively rare, to hand flat machines, which are highly versatile and admirably suited to small batch production, and power frames used in factories for large orders. These differences are related to different styles of organisation. The hand flat machines may be used in small factories or workshops or operated by individual outworkers, whereas the power frames are used by the firms with substantial factory accommodation and, at the other extreme, handknitting is restricted to a few individuals who operate independently. This variety and fragmentation in the organisation of the industry (with turnovers ranging from less than £5,000 to more than £100,000) makes it difficult to achieve coordination, notably in the field of marketing. It has been argued that rationalisation should be encouraged with greater concentration around a few large firms in Lerwick and Scalloway, and that no further new firms be assisted unless their activities are clearly based on additional labour reserves or relate to special circumstances. The number of firms is now falling after the tremendous expansion of the late 1960s, but for the present the industry will have to cope with a wide range of interest groups. A strong manufacturers' association is vital, but the precedents are not too encouraging. The Shetland Woollen Industry Association was formed in 1921, but it failed to get the unqualified support of the industry and proved effective only in times of crisis. In 1968 the Shetland Knitwear Manufacturers' Association was formed and although 'enthusiasm has not been universal', it remains to be seen whether some agreement can be found over stamping and labelling which will be a sure indication of quality and remove the ambiguity over the origin of the product. This is particularly important for export prospects. About three-quarters of total production is exported, mostly to Europe and North America.[43]

A further problem concerns the wool supply. It has been calculated that Shetland sheep (including selected crosses) could produce no more than 80,000kg of pure yarn. Not only is this far below the needs of the industry at present (about 180,000kg per annum) but the wool in its pure state is too delicate, and commercial production is best served by blending Shetland wool with other types. From the 1890s it has been customary to send Shetland clip to the mainland, Brora especially, where spinning and blending is carried out. The wool returned to the island seldom has a 'Shetland' content of more than 20 per cent. A corollary of this practice is that Shetland wool is blended into yarns supplied to other firms in Scotland and, indeed, to customers abroad, notably in France and Italy. Although the 'Shetland' content in these wools is nominal, there is some justification for regarding it as Shetland wool and advertising the products manufactured from it accordingly. The ambiguity thus arising between Shetland as a wool source and a place of knitwear manufacture may be deliberately fostered by Shetland's competitors, but clarification might have come from the Shetland industry in the event of greater singlemindedness over basic policy issues. A good deal of discussion in recent years has focused on the desirability of a spinning mill in Shetland. Such a mill would avoid the need for despatch of local wool to mainland mills, and at the same time it would allow greater contact between the processing of Shetland wool and the island-based knitting industry. This could be a valuable asset since greater standardisation might be possible, ensuring that the specified proportions of different wools were maintained. However, it is unlikely that enough wool would be available to justify the entire yarn production sequence to be carried out in Shetland and the inadequacy of Shetland wool alone (in terms of quality and quantity) would require the import of other wools from outside and the export of part of the blended wool output. This export of Shetland wool would thereby perpetuate the ambiguity behind the 'Shetland' label. Also some Shetland firms expressed their confidence in the mainland mills and indicated their intention of retaining their business links even if a new mill were to be built on the island. Thus the ideal of retaining wool within Shetland is quite unrealistic. But although enmeshed in a political web spun by the various local interest groups, the saga of the spinning mill is an interesting case study in demonstrating the constraints affecting island industrial locations. Even where the raw material is available on the island and most of the product aimed at the local consumers, there are problems due to the unacceptably small scale of production, the partial dependence on outside sources for raw materials and the difficulty of capturing present business links forged with the mainland by both wool producers and yarn buyers.

The problems of the Highlands are local expressions of a process of innovation evident throughout the Scottish textile industry. Technical change has brought greater efficiency and substantial falls in employment (Table 5). The contraction has not brought high unemployment for it is evident from Fig 9 (see

(see p42) that most textile manufacturing areas have unemployment rates consistently below the Scottish average. The
problem of redundancy has been solved largely by migration and
industrial diversification, although a greater effort in
retraining seems to be needed. The time of writing is one of
particular uncertainty in the industry. Redundancy and short-
time working is evident in the jute industry, where mills
continue to close and long-term doubts about the future of
the crop in famine-torn Bangladesh hang over the trade.
Polypropylene has been hit by the recession in the tufted
carpet business, and a catastrophic fall in demand for high-
quality garments has hit the Border woollen industry,
particularly the Braeburn Group, so prominent in the Hawick
hosiery trade. However, many firms continue to take an
optimistic view over the longer term and continuing diversification will reduce the local effects of future recessions.

Table 5

EMPLOYMENT IN THE TEXTILE INDUSTRY 1951-71

Region	1951 Textiles			1951 Clothing			1961 Textiles			1961 Clothing			1971 Textiles			1971 Clothing		
	M	F	Total	M	F	Total	M	F	Total	M	F	Total	M	F	Total	M	F	Total
Highland	1.83	0.78	2.61	0.14	0.18	0.32	1.96	0.68	2.64	0.03	0.12	0.15	1.84	0.63	2.47	0.03	0.29	0.32
Grampian	1.48	3.27	4.75	0.35	0.79	1.14	1.73	2.73	4.46	0.05	0.13	0.18	1.97	2.45	4.42	0.08	0.40	0.48
Tayside	11.74	14.95	26.69	0.45	1.58	2.03	10.58	10.93	21.51	0.26	0.84	1.10	8.28	7.03	15.31	0.26	0.74	1.00
NORTH	15.05	19.00	34.05	0.94	2.55	3.49	14.27	14.34	28.61	0.34	1.09	1.43	12.09	10.11	22.20	0.37	1.43	1.80
Borders	5.66	5.86	11.52	0.12	0.27	0.39	5.84	6.88	12.72	0.02	0.17	0.19	5.30	5.37	10.67	0.07	0.15	0.22
Dumfries & Galloway	0.48	1.78	2.26	0.08	0.16	0.24	0.68	1.61	2.29	*	0.05	0.05	0.82	1.74	2.56	0.12	0.75	0.87
SOUTH	6.14	7.64	13.78	0.20	0.43	0.63	6.52	8.49	15.01	0.02	0.22	0.24	6.12	7.11	13.23	0.19	0.90	1.09
OUTER REGIONS	21.19	26.64	47.83	1.14	2.98	4.12	20.79	22.83	43.62	0.36	1.31	1.67	18.21	17.22	35.23	0.56	2.33	2.89
CENTRAL BELT	22.80	46.93	69.73	6.34	26.20	32.54	18.88	35.58	54.46	3.97	19.75	23.72	16.04	24.66	40.70	3.88	24.22	28.10
SCOTLAND	43.99	73.57	117.56	7.48	29.18	36.66	39.67	58.41	98.08	4.33	21.06	25.39	34.25	41.88	76.13	4.44	26.45	30.99

All figures in '000s
* less than 0.01

Source: Census of Scotland - Industry and Status Tables (based on a 10 per cent sample)

3

Bladnoch to Highland Park:
the Scotch Whisky Record

The food and drink sector has already been noted for its strong
contribution to the economy of the Outer Regions. There is
considerable diversity, extending to fish processing, fruit
preserving and milk manufacturing (including butter, cheese
and condensed milk), as well as to bakery products and quality
canned foods, exemplified by such extended family businesses
as Douglas of Selkirk (now Border Bakeries) and Baxters of
Fochabers respectively.[1] However, in the interests of coherence
this chapter is restricted to Scotch whisky, romanticised by
such emotive brand names as 'Dew of Ben Nevis' and by innumer-
able publications so crammed with colourful tales of smuggling
and illicit distillation that distilling may well be regarded
as the most traditional of all Highland industries. It is
interesting to speculate that the art of distillation was
brought to Scotland by the Crusaders who had come into contact
with Arab traders familiar with Chinese culture. But there is
firmer evidence of the production of this fine liquor among
medieval monastic communities, where it was regarded as Aqua
Vitae, 'water of life' (the Gaelic equivalent is 'Uisge Beatha'
and the word 'whisky' probably develops as a corruption of
this). The association with the monasteries is brought out in
Morayshire, where the Miltonduff distillery draws water from
the Black Burn, formerly blessed by the abbot of the Pluscarden
community: the life-giving beverage proved so good that it
'made the hearts of all rejoice and filled the abbey with
unutterable bliss'.[2] Originally, however, only beer was made.
The earliest recorded evidence of whisky in Scotland comes from
the Exchequer Rolls of 1494, but by this time it is very
likely that production was widespread in all parts of the ,
country, possibly originating in Kintyre where travellers from
Ireland would have made their landfall.

    The production process begins with the soaking of malting
barley (high in starch content) in water, followed by spreading

68

out on a malting floor where the barley grows for a period of some ten days, being turned over periodically during this time. Germination converts the starch in the barley into sugary maltose. This saccharified grain, or malt, is then dried over a peat fire to arrest the sprouting process and implant a distinctive aroma. The hard dry grains may then be milled into grist and mashed in hot water to give a sugary liquid (wort) to which yeast will be added, yielding, after a period of one to three days, a weak alcohol called wash. Meanwhile, the malt residue is abstracted and either sold off as draff for cattle feed or else incorporated with other distillery effluents in a manufacturing process for animal feed. The wash is then subject to two distillations, the first yielding 'low wines' and the second potable spirit. The distillation process is, however, far from simple and requires careful monitoring of temperature and density, achieved by the use of instruments today but formerly done by careful assessment of taste and smell. Only the 'middle cut' (perhaps less than half the distillation) is acceptable: progress is monitored in a spirit safe and undesirable fusil oils detected when the distillate turns blue with the addition of water. The oily foreshots and the tailings or feints are retained for further distillation along with the next input of low wines. Although the whisky was once drunk straight from the barrel, it has been found to improve in quality if it is allowed to mature in casks, preferably in used sherry casks, for a period of several years. The legal minimum to allow the potable spirit to qualify as Scotch whisky is three years, but gains in smoothness continue up to the twelve-year mark, observed by many distilleries. Some whisky is kept for an even longer period, although the gain in quality is slower. After the completion of the maturing period the whisky is diluted to the acceptable proof standard and either bottled as a straight malt whisky or else blended with other malts on a grain whisky base.[3]

Expressed in such cryptic terms the production process may seem simple and straightforward, capable of being followed anywhere at any particular scale of manufacture. However, the malt whisky from pot stills, essential to all brands of Scotch, not only varies considerably in taste from one distillery to another but has proved notoriously difficult to imitate outside Scotland. The Scottish climate is important, especially during the maturing period: soft air permeates the casks and eliminates undesirable constituents at a rate appropriate to the production of a mellow whisky. But most important is the water, for a supply of good, soft peaty water is essential to a distillery. A mains supply would be quite unacceptable. These factors also

help to explain why malt whisky varies considerably between
distilleries Water seems to be the decisive factor, for
neighbouring distilleries with different water supply sources
are known to produce whiskies quite dissimilar in flavour.
However, the size and shape of the stills is also important as
is the precise method of production: the art of distilling, as
evolved at any one distillery, must be carefully emulated in
the interests of consistency, for once the unique qualities of
the whisky of a particular distillery have been appreciated
they must apply at all times. However, it has proved possible
to generalise about the characteristics of malt whiskies drawn
from different parts of the country. A line from Greenock to
Dundee separates the Highland malt whiskies from their
relatively mild Lowland counterparts. All the Lowland malt
distilleries except one are in the Central Belt. Although many
Highland malts have a forceful peaty flavour, there are some
with more subtle characteristics and a fine 'bouquet' bearing
some affinities with Lowland malts, for example Old Pulteney
(Wick), Mortlach-Glenlivet, and, most of all perhaps,
Glenmorangie, a particularly gentle and delicate whisky. Then,
in a special category come the heavier peatier malts of south
Argyll, known under the name of Islay/Campbeltown malts. This
area does not, however, extend to Oban, where the whisky has a
unique character difficult to classify in any of the three
main divisions. The qualities of all three main types of whisky
are appreciated by the blenders, and this means that not only
do the Outer Regions retain a strong interest in the country's
whisky industry but the distribution within the country is
stabilised within limits.[4]

The Formative Period

     Until the late eighteenth century, ale was the common
beverage and much of the whisky drunk in the Highlands was
imported from the South. The upper echelons of Highland society
inclined towards claret, duty-free until 1780, or else to rum
and brandy, quantities of which were smuggled in through the
free port of the Isle of Man to Kintyre and the Solway, or
brought to the North Isles by the Dutch fishing fleet. Not
that distillation was totally absent. In 1690 the Scottish
parliament made a special grant to Duncan Forbes of Culloden
as compensation for the ravaging of his estates by angry
Jacobites retaliating against Forbes's assistance in the over-
throw of James II. He was granted the privilege of distilling
grain on his estate free of duty (apart from a small annual
sum excise levy, initially £22 but rising to £73 by 1781 when
about 100,000 gallons was produced, so much that his 'Ferintosh'

became a synonym for whisky).[5] There was much displeasure at
the vast profit, for the whisky was sold on both sides of the
border and a warehouse was opened in London in 1780 to handle
the growing demand there, but the privilege was withdrawn only
when the 1784 legislation came in. By this time whisky was
being consumed at breakfast in fashionable households, and was
rivalling imported spirits as an acceptable after-dinner drink.
As Youngson comments, the distilling of whisky came to absorb
'an increasing amount of highland, barley, time and ingenuity'.[6]
Tastes were evidently changing, but it is also evident that
agricultural output was increasing and the export of the
surplus production in the form of whisky gave worthwhile
rewards. Thus the minister of Killearnan parish (Ross &
Cromarty) wrote that 'distilling is almost the only method of
converting our victual into cash for the payment of rent and
servants and whisky may, in fact, be called our staple
commodity'.[7]

Properly regulated, the distilling industry could have
brought considerable prosperity and accelerated agricultural
improvements. But the taxation system brought many complications.
Government was naturally apprehensive about increasing whisky
consumption, and saw heavy duties as both a source of wealth
and a curb on excessive drinking. Their legislation, however,
had also to take some cognisance of the existing Lowland
distillery trade in both the Central Belt and London at this
time of expansion in the Highlands: the southern distillers
stood to lose out to the malt whisky from Scotland. Apart from
Ferintosh, a particular bone of contention, malt whisky could
either be produced in licensed distilleries or manufactured
illicitly, in the case of many individual operators of small
stills who did not confine their production to their own use.
The illicit whisky competed successfully because of price and
quality advantages. It was made entirely from malt whereas
licensed distilleries, liable to the malt tax, tried to reduce
their liabilities by introducing as much as 80 per cent of raw
grain. The illicit export trade must have been small in the
early 1780s, but the kegs of whisky carried by ponies over the
hills and bartered in southern markets acted as a modest
stimulus to the northern economy and seems to have been
considered damaging by established distillers there.

The result was a new Distillery Act, which took effect in
1786.[8] Government tried to help the licensed distillers while
at the same time recognising that it would be unrealistic to
impose a uniform system right across the country: Highland
operating conditions were more difficult and uncertain while

administration was also complicated. The Highland case for the
legal recognition of small stills was accepted. The legalising
of production at all levels above 20-gallon still capacity
made it quite legitimate to supply barley to small distilleries,
and this stimulated agricultural development. The new act also
helped the Highlands by recognising that its output per unit
of still capacity tended to be lower and that its harvests were
more variable. Taxation per unit of capacity was therefore set
at a lower level than the £1.50 levied in the Lowlands
(reckoned to be 2½p per gallon of whisky produced). But this
implied a clear administrative boundary marking off the area
of the Highland distillery; not only was it forbidden for
cereals to cross the boundary, but Highland whisky was not to
be sold in the Lowlands except on payment of additional duties.
Furthermore, to help the London distillers, liable to a tax
of 12p per gallon of spirits produced, any whisky exports to
England would carry an equalising duty of 10p per gallon. The
increase in this duty to 12p in 1788 was a further incentive
to illicit distilling and smuggling. Even within Scotland,
rising rates of duty in the 1790s meant a difference in retail
price of rather more than 10 per cent above the illegal product.
This seems trivial in relation to current levels of duty, but
it proved enough to stimulate the illegal operator, especially
during the war years 1795-7 when all distillation was forbidden,
to conserve grain. Local dissatisfaction with the legal system
in the late eighteenth century is clearly evident from the
pages of the Statistical Account. The minister at Kirkhill
(Inverness) considered that 'the consumption of barley by the
distilleries made the price of grain very high for the poor
people, while the barriers to the export of whisky meant a
copious supply within the parish, tempting local people to
drink at low prices in the dram-houses, condemned as "seminaries
of vice and idleness" '.[9] The illegal distillation of whisky
continued, and it benefited considerably from the sympathatic
attitude of magistrates and of landlords who were well aware
of the benefits of having a local market for barley. However,
some were far-sighted enough to realise that the constant need
for vigilance consumed energies which could have been better
used in productive work, while the bitter experience of a
detection could be demoralising enough to inhibit further
enterprise. The need for secluded locations meant that squatting
took place on the margins of estates and a regular plan of
improvement could not easily be implemented.[10]

On the Gordon estates in Moray, illegal distillation was
particularly prominent. The fashion was evidently not long-
established for the minister of Mortlach refers to the drinking

of whisky, instead of good ale, as a 'miserable change' and together with 'the very general use of tea' was evidently proving 'hurtful both to health and morals'.[11] The expansion in the number of tea kettles was paralleled by the growth of illicit distilleries, most numerous in Glenlivet. This glen lay away from the principal military highways, yet the tracks over the Ladder Hills and Mounth afforded a tenuous contact with its markets and there was ample water, with numerous headwaters draining into the airy Braes of Glenlivet where former shieling grounds proved capable of conversion to arable land. The highly fragmented settlement pattern, clearly brought out on late eighteenth-century estate maps, did not conform with the model of neatness and regularity which improving landlords were seeking to apply, and it was not at all inappropriate that the Duke of Gordon, anxious to extend his estate developments from the Huntly and Tomintoul areas towards Glenlivet, Mortlach and Cabrach, should have petitioned the government strongly over distillery policy. His aim was to control the industry by strong sanctions against illegal operators combined with moderate taxation for licensed premises. According to D. Bremner, government pressure on landowners to use their authority to suppress illicit distillation drew the reply from the Duke of Gordon that he and his colleagues would comply 'if the Legislature would pass an Act affording an opening for the manufacture of whisky as good as the smuggled product at a reasonable rate of duty payable'.[12] The outcome was the legislation of 1823 which required a £10 licence fee on each still (minimum capacity 40 gallons) and levied a duty of only 11p on each gallon of proof spirit (compared with 47p imposed in 1815). The new act also assisted the industry by allowing whisky to be stored duty free in bonded warehouses during the maturation period. Superior whisky could be legally marketed in the South, and numerous new licensed distilleries were started. George Smith took out a license for his bothy business at Upper Drumin, Glenlivet, and gradually raised his production from 50 to 200 gallons each week, exporting his whisky through the Moray ports of Burghead and Garmouth. The demand for barley was satisfied by the nearby farms of Castletown, Nevie and Minmore which Smith leased and improved. After a fire at Drumin in 1858 he relocated his distillery at Minmore where the core of the present Glenlivet distillery was built.

The act was necessarily unpopular to many distillers since their stills were too small to qualify. For some years bands of Glenlivet men maintained a futile resistence, trudging South via the Ladder Trail to meet bitter encounters with the

excisemen in Glenbuchat and Strathdon where the forces of law
were supported by the military garrison at Corgarff. Illegal
distillation had virtually ceased by the 1840s, when the
minister for Inveravon (Moray), of which Glenlivet was part,
reported that people were 'happily and successfully employed
in the cultivation of farms or in prosecuting handicrafts',
the example of the more skilful and opulent tenants being
readily imitated.[13] Some individual cases continued to achieve
a degree of notoriety. There were elaborate measures taken up
the Coryhabbie Burn in Glen Rinnes where water was diverted
round the face of Muckle Laprach to a secluded base where
whisky would be produced with impunity. 'Malt caves' in the
hills were a refuge for germination, while distilled whisky
was hidden in pits dug in the hillside and camouflaged with
heather, prior to distribution along the Moray coast (concealed
in transit by less controversial lines of farm produce).[14]
The Beldorney gamekeeper distilled whisky in Glass parish
throughout his working life and was only checked by the excise
through indiscretions in his old age. Persistent smugglers
could carry on for decades with elaborate warning systems and
ingenious means of dissipating smoke. They would re-equip by
surrendering old equipment in a specially prepared decoy bothy
and use the financial reward for disclosing information to the
authorities to buy new 'plant'. But the illegal operator
became increasingly isolated. His seclusion was eroded by
progressive improvements in communications, and whereas the
illicit product was far superior to the 'Parliament whisky'
before 1823, it was difficult in later years even for the most
skilled distiller to compete with the licensed stills. It
needed the greatest care to ensure that the liquid collected
as whisky was free of harmful impurities, and the cramped bothy
could hardly match the sophistication of the major distillers.
Certainly in the late nineteenth century such circumstances as
the excisemen's restraint in deer forests during the stalking
season, the crofters immunity from eviction after 1886, even
with conviction for smuggling and the requirement of proof of
actual distilling (and not just malting, as was the case prior
to 1880), all helped marginally to encourage illicit distillation. But whatever romantic appeal isolated lawlessness might
have, the detection rate, running at around twenty per annum
in the 1880s, is insignificant compared with the hundreds of
casualties in the early 1820s. In short, although the
vigilance of the excisemen was not an insuperable constraint,
the uncertainty of the business and capital shortage forced
the illicit industry into perpetual retreat.[15]

Some distilleries still operating today were licensed

before the 1823 act. Strathisla-Glenlivet distillery at Keith
dates back to 1786 and Balblair (Ross & Cromarty), Glengarioch
(Gordon) and Highland Park (Orkney) were all open by the end
of the century. In the early nineteenth century came Clynelish
in Brora, Glenburgie near Forres and Millburn in Inverness.
But there was a very substantial response to the new act. By
the end of 1824 there was a distillery on Mull at Tobermory,
and other units in the Grampian region at Banff, Bennachie
(Insch), and Fettercairn, besides the Speyside distilleries at
Belmenanch, Cardow, Macallan, Miltonduff — and Mortlach, the
first of Dufftown's 'seven stills'. In the late 1820s new
openings included Blair Atholl (Perth & Kinross), Glendronach
(Gordon), Old Pulteney (Wick) and Royal Lochnagar on Deeside
and developments in the 1830s confirm the impression of a wide
locational spread: Ben Rinnes and Glenfarclas (Moray),
Glenury (Stonehaven) and Talisker (Skye & Lochalsh). Certainly
the areas notorious for illicit distillation developed a
licensed trade, as at Lagavulin on Islay (Argyll), where the
precious output of 'Moonlight' had previously come from small
bothies, or at Blair Atholl where it was no doubt 'the
mellowed barley bree from the caverns of Ben Vrackie that
warmed the hearts and strengthened the arms of the Highlanders
at Killiecrankie'.[16] But many other locations are involved
where there cannot have been very much local expertise. Market
towns with their own local barley supply and an acceptable
water source feature quite prominently. The main emphasis was
in the North but Dumfries & Galloway experienced a boom:
Bladnoch (Merrick) is the sole survivor of a group of ten
units scattered across the region by 1850. The only significant
concentration in the early nineteenth century was in Campbeltown
(Argyll & Bute). The first licensed distillery was opened in
1815, but there were fourteen units by 1836, when reference
was made to improvements in quality making the Campbeltown
whisky competitive with the Islay product 'to which it has
been hitherto considered inferior'.[17] Just a few years later
twenty-five distilleries are mentioned in the town with
whisky of excellent quality the 'great staple commodity'.
Output ran at 0.75 million gallons, and capital was being fed
into the industry by merchants who had previously invested in
fishing. Supported by the principal barley lands of Kintyre
and a vigorous local malting industry, the town was in a good
situation to supply Glasgow: 'the easy and perpetual intercourse
by steam-boats has brought the market to its doors'.[18]

The Impact of Grain Whisky

The rapid expansion of the industry after the new deal

of 1823, reflected in the growth period of the 1820s and 1830s, gave way to decades of more restrained growth. The industry was weakened by increases in duty to 14p in 1826, 17p in 1830 and 18p in 1840, but these modest rises were followed by much steeper increases to 23p in 1853, 30p in 1854, 40p in 1855 and 50p in 1860. The late 1850s was a period of sharp contraction in the number of malt whisky distilleries. Another reason why malt whisky encountered mixed fortunes in the mid-century lay in the competition experienced from grain whisky. The process uses some malted barley, but it is mixed with unmalted rye and maize, cooked under steam pressure. The starch cells in the grain burst, and in the mash tun the diastase of the malted barley converts the starch into sugar. Further processing is also different because instead of intermittent distillation in pot stills, the grain whisky distiller employs a continuous process using the large patent still, first produced by Robert Stein in the 1820s for the Kilbagie distillery at Kincardine (Fife) and then improved in 1830 by a retired Irish excise officer, Aeneas Coffey. Grain whisky is more uniform in character and relatively cheap to produce. Combined with its mild flavour, in contrast to the relatively robust and over-powering malts, grain whisky became highly competitive, especially in urban areas. In 1857 total production of malt whisky was 5.47 million gallons, compared with 5.41 for grain, but the decline due to rising taxation was far greater for malt than grain so that comparable figures for 1867 were 4.77 and 5.32 respectively. By this time the popularity of the grain whisky had increased through blending malt whiskies into it, a process pioneered by Andrew Usher in Edinburgh during the 1850s and early 1860s.

Some new distilleries opened in the middle years of the nineteenth century. The Glen Grant distillery opened in Rothes in 1840, Glenmorangie was first distilled in 1843 in converted brewery premises near Tain (Ross & Cromarty) and Coal Isla (Islay) went on stream in 1846, the same year as the Glen Albyn distillery in Inverness. However, even during the growth period there were some closures. The Langholm distillery in the Dumfries & Galloway region, opened in 1786, closed in 1826.[19] Apparently there were acute capital shortages due to the heavy financial burden of warehousing whisky during the maturation period. But this problem, especially if combined with managerial weaknesses or a relatively unpopular product, would have been more debilitating in later years. J. Black commented that closures in the industry resulted from 'men rushing into business who had not sufficient knowledge of it nor capital to carry it on'.[20] But there was a general problem of 'formidable

competition' from the great distilleries of the Central Belt
which turned out 'a coarser and cheaper spirit than, in the
circumstances of the distillers here (in Moray), can be
produced'.[21] The records are too sketchy to make accurate
assessments of regional variations in the extent of distillery
closure. But some small units in remote parts of the Grampian
uplands at Blackmiddens (Cabrach) and Lesmurdie disappeared in
the years after the New Statistical Account was written, with
similar demographic consequences to the earlier suppression of
illicit distillation: families removed to the towns and other
parishes after a period of growth when whisky profits had
maintained them 'among the hills and valleys'. The island
distilleries of Lewis all failed: Coll, Gress and Shoeburn
(Stornoway), although the industry survived in Islay and Skye,
whisky being sent out by puffer to the Central Belt. The
influence of the distilleries on agricultural improvement was
an important consideration. The distilleries of Muthill (Perth
& Kinross) were 'advantageous in the consumption of the grain
and the feeding of cattle and the manuring of the ground, as
also in employing many workmen'. Indeed there was 'much to be
applauded in everything except the object for which it is
made'.[22] Some decades later D. Barnard, reporting on his visit
to Royal Lochnagar distillery, wrote of the hundred head of
fine cattle which consumed the draff and spent wash, and
mentioned the farmlands, stretching almost to Abergeldie, which
'produce splendid barley and grain'.[23] How then was agriculture
affected by distillery closures? Perhaps improved transport and
greater regional specialisation reduced the significance of
local (distillery) markets? In Barnard's time many distilleries
had outstripped local resources and were forced to bring barley
in. Thus Glenlivet still disposed of draff locally, but barley
came by rail to Ballindalloch and was carted from there to the
distillery, while the distillery on Mull had to import barley
by steamer from the Moray coastlands.[24]

Naturally, malt whisky interests were opposed to the
rival grain whisky, although they were unsuccessful in their
bid to have such manufacture declared illegal. They were
equally unsuccessful in their opposition to blending, or the
'adulteration' of putting grain whisky into malt and referring
to the blends as 'Highland whisky'. Blending, however, is a
highly skilled business. Certain whiskies are mutually
incompatible and the malts must, therefore, be selected so as
to emphasise the desired characteristics. Then, 'the malts and
grains in a blend must be chosen to complement and enhance
their respective flavours. Thus blending is in no sense a
dilution but the combining of like with like, to produce a

whisky that brings out the best qualities of each of its
constituent parts.' Timing is also important, for once the
blend has been built up on paper, the cask sampled and the
whiskies mixed, or roused, in a blending vat, the whisky is
put back into wood and left to 'marry' for an appropriate
period. Finally, once a blend with a definite character has
been developed this has to be retained with the utmost consistency. Scientific instruments may reveal the chemistry, but
the blender has to rely ultimately on 'a mental image that
brings back a taste or a smell' to recognise the magic formula.
Few individual grain whiskies are needed, but as many as forty
different malts may be used. Blending tended to improve the
uniformity of Scotch whisky. Previously it was not easy for the
consumer to tell whether he was getting grain or malt, and if
the latter, whether it was highly or moderately flavoured.
Consequently the less-variable Irish whisky was often preferred.
Grain whisky could thus be seen as an advantage for the whole
industry, maintaining the quality and taste of the malt whisky
and greatly increasing quantity. At home the eclipse of rival
drinks: brandy, gin and rum in the 1880s gave blended whisky
'the key of the situation'. But blended whiskies were also
highly acceptable by people in sedentary occupations in warmer
climates abroad; Scotch became more competitive on the
continent when supplies of cognac were reduced by the ravages
of phylloxera.

Paradoxically, however, the legal skirmishing lasted for
decades and was not finally terminated until a Royal Commission
reported in 1909 with the simple pronouncement that 'whisky is
a spirit obtained by distillation from a mash of cereal grains
saccharified by the diastase of malt'.[25] The legal recognition
for blended whisky implied by this decision was not really
harmful to the malt producers, although they suffered from
injured pride through their product, a work of art, being given
no clear status over the 'tasteless' grain product. The late
nineteenth century was a period of expansion. In 1877, 7.16
million gallons of malt whisky was produced and 11.38 million
gallons of grain. Twenty years later the figures were 13.98
and 17.30 respectively. The greater expansion for malt whisky
than grain, 95.4 per cent compared with 52.0, indicates how
much the malt whisky trade revived as a result of blending
techniques and the decline in sales of straight grain whisky,
directly in competition with malt. Many new distilleries were
built. Some of the new units were outside the main production
areas: Linkwood (Elgin) 1873, Glen Rothes 1878, Ben Nevis
(Fort William) 1878, Ben Wyvis (Dingwall) 1879. The year 1881
saw two new distilleries on Islay, Bruichladdich and

Bunnahabhain, and Scapa distillery opened in Orkney in 1885
and Glen Mhor (Inverness) in 1892. But the greatest growth took
place on Speyside, and although many new distilleries were
built after his tour, Barnard's record, summarised in Table 6,
shows that the Moray district had a prominent position. Islay
and Campbeltown still had a large number of distilleries, and
it was said that the bouquet from the latter's stills was
strong enough to constitute a real aid to navigation in foggy
weather'. Frcm researches by M. C. Storrie it emerges that there
was a reduction of nearly half in the total number of distilleries from 259 in 1833 to 131 in 1887, but net reductions in
the Grampian and Highland regions were relatively slight.[26]
Apart from the Central Belt, the sharpest decline came in
Tayside. It would seem that the less highly flavoured malts
from these areas were suffering heavy competition, but the
question needs further examination The Central Belt units were
relatively large, leaving aside the grain distilleries, and
such possibilities as competition for labour and water with
other industries need consideration in interpreting regional
trends.

At Glenlivet, Barnard had longed for the skills of an
artist 'to enable us to transfer to canvas this scene of
majestic grandeur'[27] and it is not unreasonable to speculate
that his enthusiasm for the area helped to instill a longing
for the 'traditional' products of the heather hills. But there
were other location factors working in Speyside's interests.
The area enjoyed a high reputation among the blenders, and the
'Glenlivet' whisky, originally produced first by the illicit
operators and later by George Smith at Drumin, came to express
the general character of the region. A legal battle in 1880 led
to the Glenlivet whisky being differentiated from the products
of all the other distilleries in the area which have linked
Glenlivet to their names. With ample water supplies, the
capacity of Speyside for whisky production proved very
considerable. It has been pointed out that the flanks of the
Cairngorms, drained by the Deveron, Spey and Findhorn and their
tributaries, provide very suitable water especially in the
'golden rectangle' drawn around Ben Rinnes between Aberlour/
Craigellachie, Dufftown, Glenlivet and Ballindalloch where
water drains off peaty moors developed on granites and
granulites.[28] Although there are several distilleries around
Keith in an area of schists, limestone bands here are believed
to affect the quality of the water. Speyside also enjoyed good
access to the barley fields of the Laich of Moray once local
resources had been outstripped. Furthermore, the area was
connected with the Aberdeen–Inverness railway by the branch

Table 6

WHISKY DISTILLERIES 1887 AND 1973

Region	1887 Grain Whisky a	b	c	1887 Malt Whisky* a	b	c	1973 Grain Whisky a	b	c	1973 Malt Whisky a	b	c	Share of Prodn (per cent) d	e	f
Highland				53	4.89	0.09	2	11.50	5.75	31	21.56	0.70	44.2	9.9	26.3
Argyll District only				34	3.49	0.10				12	6.62	0.55	31.5		8.1
Grampian				32	2.96	0.09				58	48.63	0.84	59.3		59.3
Moray District only				19	1.57	0.08				48	43.78	0.91	14.2		53.4
Tayside				9	0.43	0.05	1	0.80	0.80	9	3.89	0.43	3.9	0.7	4.7
NORTH				94	8.23	0.09	3	12.30	4.10	98	74.08	0.76	74.3	10.6	90.4
Borders															
Dumfries & Galloway				4	0.20	0.05				1	0.60	0.60	1.8		0.7
SOUTH				4	0.20	0.05				1	0.60	0.60	1.8		0.7
OUTER REGIONS				98	8.43	0.09	3	12.30	4.10	99	74.68	0.75	76.2	10.6	91.1
CENTRAL BELT	11	12.85	1.17	21	2.64	0.13	11	113.80	10.35	12	7.26	0.60	23.8	89.4	8.9
SCOTLAND	11	12.85	1.17	119	11.07	0.09	14	116.10	8.29	111	81.94	0.74			

* Includes some grain whisky in distilleries producing both types
(a) Number of distilleries; (b) total production (1887); estimated capacity (1973) (million gallons); (c) average production/
capacity (million gallons) per distillery; (d) 1887 malt whisky; (e) 1973 grain whisky, (f) 1973 malt whisky

Sources: Barnard, A. The Whisky Distilleries of the UK (London: Harper's Gazette, 1887); Glass, B.W. and Shakerley, C.F.E.
Scotch Whisky (London: Roger Mortimer, 1973)

line from Keith to Dufftown, later extended along Strathspey to Aberlour, Grantown and Aviemore. Expansion in this area continues at the present time, not only by enlargements at individual distilleries, but by new building at Tormore, Tomintoul–Glenlivet, Tomnavoulin–Glenlivet, the Braes of Glenlivet and Glenallochy–Aberlour. The late nineteenth century distilleries were built close to the railways, leaving the older units to adapt to the new means of transport by either building branch lines to the works (as at Balmenach and Dailuaine) or by carting produce to and from the nearest station. Now, with the emphasis back on road transport, there is greater flexibility, and the newest of distilleries are tapping water supplies in relatively inaccessible areas.

Modern Trends

The late nineteenth–century boom reached its climax in 1898 with the failure of the blending firm of Pattison Brothers whose ostentatious advertising proved to be recklessly extravagant. World War I restrictions on grain supply created difficulties. Also to be contended with were discriminatory taxes levied in foreign markets. Scotch did infiltrate the American market during the Prohibition period, and it gained a measure of popularity which was advantageous when restrictions were removed in 1933. But by that year the depression had helped to reduce the number of distilleries in operation to less than twenty (compared with rather more than 120 in 1920). By 1940 the total had been restored to approximately ninety, but further wartime shortages, although held off for as long as possible, brought production to a complete standstill by 1944. Creeping back to full output by 1948, the industry embarked on record export business which, until well into the 1950s, resulted in shortages on the home market.[29] In 1972, exports amounted to 68.76 million gallons and the home consumption to only 12.58.[30] Present production shows a considerable margin over sales, but the latter concerns mature whisky: present production will, of course, sell in the future when demand is expected to be greater. The home market has been hard hit by sharp increase in duty. World War I shortages brought the level to £3.62 per gallon, advancing slightly to £3.85 by 1939. The rise has continued from £11.60 in 1948 to £17.68 in 1968 and £22.09 in 1975. However, home sales have shown a slow expansion and the market is a profitable one for the producer. Blended whiskies remain very popular, but the rise in sales also affect the straight malt whiskies. Indeed, some distilleries have had to buy back their whisky from blenders in order to meet increased demand. While many malt distilleries still

produce exclusively for blending, a growing number bottle
their own product, and other distillers, such as Ledaig
(Tobermory), have decided to extend their warehousing so that a
proportion of their malt can be retained for maturation and
bottling in future. Although comparatively rare south of the
border, a number of shops in Scotland stock a very wide range
of malts and each individual malt is well represented in shops
in its own area. The cost of the malts is greater than the
blended whiskies, as might be expected, since malt whisky is
approximately twice as expensive to produce as the grain whisky
which forms the bulk of the blend. However, the difference is
reduced by the cost of blending, and by the costs for bottling,
packaging and transport which exceed the total production costs
of the whisky at the vatting stage. Furthermore, the duty,
amounting to a surcharge equivalent to almost ten times the
cost of putting the whisky on the market, is charged at a
standard rate. Helped by the publicity gained through effective
advertising and provision for tourists at distilleries,
developed to a fine art by Grant's at Glenfiddich, the malt
sales are likely to increase, but it is questionable whether
they will rise at a faster rate than whisky consumption overall.

To cater for the rise in production since World War II
there have been many extensions made to existing distilleries
(Fig 11). Indeed the evidence of growth at virtually every
Speyside distillery during 1974 was most impressive and
created an atmosphere of quiet confidence. Present expansion
of malt capacity follows an earlier disproportionate rise in
grain whisky output, where the peak of 1966 was only regained
in 1972 when malt production was coming more into phase. There
remains a very substantial disparity in production, exaggerated
by the longer maturation period for malt whisky and the
marketing of some of the latter in straight malt form. However,
the usual former practice of keeping an equal balance between
grain and malt in blended whiskies is retained only by
Teacher's 'Highland Cream' and by some quality blends. It is
not unusual for the grain component to reach a proportion of
two-thirds, or even four-fifths for the cheapest blends.
Expansion consists of new bonded-warehouse accommodation,
increased still capacity and new dark grains plants for
processing draff and effluent. But new distilleries are also
a feature of the contemporary scene. To some extent the new
developments involve reopening old distilleries and construction in old distillery sites. Thus the Ledaig distillery at
Tobermory, Isle of Mull, which closed in 1944 was reopened in
1972, with the financial assistance from the HIDB. It resumed
use of the original water supply from Mishnish Lochs. Old

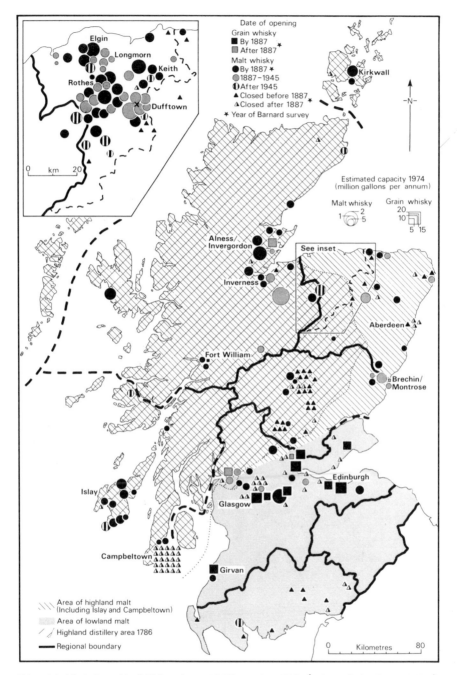

Date of opening
Grain whisky
■ By 1887
□ After 1887
Malt whisky
● By 1887
◕ 1887-1945
◖ After 1945
▲ Closed before 1887
△ Closed after 1887
✳ Year of Barnard survey

Estimated capacity 1974
(million gallons per annum)
Malt whisky
1 ◔ 2 5
Grain whisky
20 10
5 15

Area of highland malt
(Including Islay and Campbeltown)
Area of lowland malt
Highland distillery area 1786
Regional boundary

0   Kilometres   80

Fig 11 Whisky distilleries 1887 and 1973 (cf notes 2 and 31)

Pulteney distillery at Wick, which closed in 1926, was opened
again in 1951, while Bladnoch, the only distillery in South
Scotland, went on stream in 1956 after a quarter of a century's
inactivity. Port Ellen in Islay resumed production in 1967
after many years of use as a store.

The greatest demand continues to come from Speyside. The
only former distillery sites to be redeveloped in this growth
area concerns the now highly automated Caperdonich distillery
in Rothes, built in 1897 to supplement Glen Grant (to which it
was connected by pipeline) but closed in 1901 after the Pattison
crash and reopened only in 1965. The first entirely new distillery in Moray was built at Tormore near Ballindalloch between
1958 and 1960, but in recent years units have been built at
Auchroisk near Mulben and Thomshill near Elgin. The search for
good water has opened up a 'new frontier', leading the industry
further up the glens into the former strongholds of the illicit
operators. An example is the Tomintoul-Glenlivet distillery
built in 1964-5 at Ballantuam in Glen Avon after a sustained
examination of the water supply coming from a nearby spring.
But Upper Banffshire has also been host to the Tomnavoulin-
Glenlivet and Braes of Glenlivet distilleries, the latter a
highly automated unit. In such relatively remote locations,
transport costs are high but they may be set against the
market value of whisky. Although most distillery workers are
drawn from existing settlements and commute to work, there is
some reflection of the nineteenth-century 'distillery village',
characteristic of Islay and parts of Speyside, at Tormore, a
striking piece of modern industrial architecture, and at the
Braes of Glenlivet, where new housing is to be built adjacent
to the distillery site there is a great opportunity for
another impressive ensemble.

The new distilleries are not mere large-scale replicas of
the older buildings with their distinctive 'pagoda' towers.
A big change has come about through the use of centralised
maltings. Whereas individual distilleries used to handle their
own malting, spreading the barley over concrete malting floors
for germination, the usual system now involves large drum
maltings in which the process is mechanically controlled.
Mechanical malting was apparently first introduced at Glen Mhor
(Inverness). Scottish Malt Distillers operate such central
maltings at Burghead on the Moray coast and Port Ellen in
Islay, while Moray Firth Maltings have plant at Inverness and
Arbroath. Other units include Chivas Brothers at Inverboyndie
(Banff & Buchan) and Moray Firth Maltings at Arbroath and
Inverness. The new system is not only adopted by new distilleries

84

but by most of the established units which find it more economical. Valuable space is made available: distilleries in built-up areas may have considerable difficulty acquiring land for expansion. Another change is the conversion from coal to oil firing (gas in some cases) for the stills. Coal stockpiles are thus replaced by oil storage tanks, very substantial in such special cases as Talisker where fuel is obtained by sea every six months. The results of these changes are not only expressed architecturally but in employment terms.

The loss of jobs, sometimes more than a third of the total before conversion, is a serious blow in areas where little alternative employment is available. However, some additional openings arise through the installation of dark-grains plants to process draff and effluent into cattle cake. Progress has been very substantial on Speyside in the last five years. Certain distilleries have the plants built adjacent or very close to their existing premises, and these serve several distilleries which may either belong to a particular geographi-cal area, as in the case of the Combination of Rothes Distillers dark-grains plant in that town, or a particular company. Further dark-grains plants are in operation at Glenfarclas (Ballindalloch), Balvenie (Dufftown), Glenlivet, Macallan (Craigellachie) and Tomatin, and the very tall towers characteristic of these plants are becoming the most distinctive elements in the modern distillery landscape. The rate of construction has been accelerated by rising cattle-feed costs which make processing of effluent economic, combined with local surpluses of draff which cannot be exported in an unprocessed state. Pressure has also come from local authorities who have withdrawn planning permission for discharging waste on the coast at Burghead and Findochty. The only alternative is to spray effluent on moor-land, but this is expensive for the distilleries and although it can be beneficial agriculturally in converting heather moorland into reasonable grazing, the practice meets with strong reservations from river authorities concerned with pollution hazards to salmon and from local authorities worried about the condition of minor roads in experiencing heavy traffic.

The average output of individual distilleries has risen considerably. Statistics are difficult to collect since some firms will not disclose their production Hence Table 6 (see p 80) compares the estimated capacities for 1973 with the actual production figures documented by Barnard in 1887.[31] Barnard noted in some cases that production was well below capacity, although today the discrepancy between production

of 181.5 million gallons and 202.6 million estimated capacity
is fairly slight. On average, grain distilleries remain more
than ten times larger than malt distilleries, but the regional
variations in the malt category are quite considerable: the
Moray distilleries average 0.91 million gallons today, whereas
the Argyll distilleries are relatively modest at 0.55 million.
Taking individual units, the grain units range from 0.80 million
gallons for Lochside (Montrose) to 16.0 for the North British
at Edinburgh. The largest malt distillery, Tomatin with 3.25
million gallons, contrasts with Edradour (Pitlochry) at 0.15:
in 1887 Edradour was one of two distilleries producing less
than 0.01 million gallons in contrast to 0.35 from Dundashill
(Glasgow), then the largest malt distillery with stills holding
24,000 gallons compared with 'sma' stills' holding less than
500 gallons in use in the smallest distilleries.

Barnard's survey is an excellent record of the industry at
the beginning of a period of rapid growth, with great contrasts
in output and production methods. Not surprisingly many of the
smaller distilleries lacking a vigorous organisation were weeded
out by the depression of World War I and its aftermath.
However, as Edradour are quick to remind us 'a distillery need
only be big enough to produce good whisky': in this case the
small scale of output can be reconciled with profitability
through long maturation and the production of the most exclusive
blends such as 'King's Ransom', a masterpiece of whisky
production, and 'House of Lords'. Indeed a key factor in
interpreting the overall locational changes since 1887 is the
demand for the malt by the blenders. Whiskies of all types are
required in the better blends, but Glenlivet is particularly
desirable. The strong Islay whisky is especially important in
cheaper blends where malt whisky forms only a small proportion
of the total. In terms of the number of distilleries, the most
remarkable contraction has been in Campbeltown where only two
units remain. The capacity of Glen Scotia and Springbank in
1973 was estimated at 0.45 million gallons compared with a
production of 2.01 in 1887 from the thirty-two distilleries
enumerated by Barnard. The collapse came in the 1920s and, in
contrast to other areas, has proved permanent. While the small
average size of business may have been a disadvantage and
special water supplies difficult to safeguard in an urban
situation, it is also evident that the blenders have preferred
Islay as a source of heavier whiskies.[32] However, both surviving
distilleries bottle their own malts and Glen Scotia doubled
capacity in 1974.

Malt whisky thus shows a strong contrast with the brewing

industry in its continued association with many remote rural
locations, whereas the latter has been eliminated from the
Outer Regions and heavily confined to Edinburgh. Not that all
distillery locations are free from constraints on further growth.
Of course, local barley resources have long since been outstripped and there is no difficulty in bringing greater quantities
from outside. The larger amounts of fuel oil and peat can also
be supplied without any significant local constraints. A greater
problem rests with water. This is not because of any scarcity
of water in the Highlands but because of limits to the capacity
of the particular streams and springs which contribute very
greatly to the unique character of the whisky concerned.
Although other water sources, including the mains, can be used
for cooling and for processing effluent, there is no alternative
when it comes to the basic production process. Tomatin
distillery management considers that 10 million gallons is the
limit for future production, given the discharge of the Alt-
na-Frith or Free Burn. Less severe winters have reduced the
summer flow from 150,000 to 70,000 gallons an hour of which
the company already requires 30,000 to 40,000. Other distilleries have faced this problem and indeed it is partly because of
seasonal shortages of water, coupled with climatic factors,
that a 'silent season' is observed during a few weeks in
summer, although this period is also useful for maintenance of
of equipment and as a holiday period. In contrast to the malt
whisky with 91.1 per cent of capacity in the Outer Regions,
grain whisky shows an opposite bias with 89.4 per cent capacity
in the Central Belt. Since this chemically pure spirit does
not depend on unique local resources, production has gravitated
to market locations. The small proportion of capacity in the
Outer Regions is located at Fort William, Invergordon and
Montrose. These exceptional cases may be interpreted in the
context of the business structure of the industry.

Vertical integration in the industry is increasing and
this is evident in both grain and malt whisky companies and
among blenders.[33] Blending was first carried out on a small
scale by firms with no production interests, but most firms
soon found it advantageous to control some of the distilleries
whose product was incorporated in their blends. The firm of
Arthur Bell at Perth moved into blending from retail and
profited from the depression by purchasing malt distilleries
(Blair Atholl, Dufftown and Inchgower) which now supply their
central blending and bottling plant at Perth. Grain distillers
entered into a trade arrangement in 1856 and formed a fuller
union through the Distiller's Company in 1877. The company
enjoyed a virtual monopoly after the Caledonian distillery

joined the group in 1884. They moved into blending in 1898, taking advantage of the fall of Pattison Brothers of Leith to obtain suitable premises and business contacts.

In 1925 the formidable Dewar – Buchanan and Walker businesses were acquired and numerous malt-whisky distilleries, grouped in the subsidiary company Scottish Malt Distillers, were acquired during the depression. The company's very large blending and bottling business is confined to the Central Belt, including new premises at Leven (Fife). The same process may be observed at a different scale and in a different locational context in the case of Invergordon Distillers, formed in 1965 out of an amalgamation of bonding companies with the grain distillery company of Invergordon where there had been rapid growth because of shortages in the grain sector. The Highland location took advantage of development-area incentives not then available in the Central Belt, and the coastal site allowed direct shipping of maize from the continent The weakness of the individual grain producer became evident during the period of over-capacity, and in addition to the Ben Wyvis malt distillery, built on the Invergordon site in 1965, a new malt distillery was built at Tomnavoulin on Speyside (1966), and the Bruichladdich (Islay), Deanston and Tullibardine distilleries were acquired between 1969 and 1972. Blending is carried out at Invergordon where all the malts required are warehoused, but the blended whisky is shipped in bulk to Leith for bottling there.

Then there are malt-whisky interests which maintained their independence during the depression and have recently initiated a trend to vertical integration. The case of William Grant is instructive. Capital accumulated from years in employment at Mortlach distillery at Dufftown was used to take over Cardow, before building the Glenfiddich and Balvenie distilleries near Dufftown in 1887 and 1892 respectively. Some of the malt is bottled in Dufftown, but the bulk is sent to Paisley where it forms the basis of the Standfast blend. This is produced by Grants using grain whisky from Girvan where they built their own source of production in 1962 alongside their existing Ladyburn Lowland malt distillery. However, a rather smaller operator, the Ben Nevis Distillery at Fort William, preferred to expand vertically at the original malt location where grain-whisky distilling is now combined with blending and bottling 'Dew of Ben Nevis'. Other malt producers such as Glenlivet Distillers and Highland Distilleries, each with five distilleries, International Distillers & Vintners (four distilleries), Macdonald Martin Distilleries and Teacher's (two each) and Tomatin (one) now include blending. However, IDV and

Teacher's concentrate on their own blended products (Teacher's own distilling capacity is small in relation to their sales), whereas the other companies sell in bulk to other blenders as the main part of their business. None of the companies have their own grain distillery, although some of the blending houses have a call on the North British grain distillery built by Andrew Usher in 1887 to provide a grain-whisky supply independent of the Distiller's company All blending and bottling is done in the Central Belt. Finally it is evident that there is only a limited extension into malting: most of the benefits from vertical integration occur at the forward end of the production chain, so distilleries tend to move into blending and yet undertake less of their own malting. Some groups, notably DCL, have their own bulk maltings, but other companies are happy to buy malt provided it is of acceptable quality, especially since the character of the whisky depends primarily on the production process and the water supply.

Conclusion

The whisky business is large and expanding. There are several activities which depend very closely on the industry for their survival. The peat industry, represented by organisations such as Islay Peat Developments Ltd, supplies the traditional fuel still required for malt production. Large diggings have been opened up, a notable example being on the moorland edge of Dallas parish (Moray) by the road from Forres to Knockando on Speyside: peats are stacked beside the trenches to dry and then conveyed by a monorail system to a loading gantry where lorries are filled. Copper stills are supplied by specialists such as the Morayshire Copper Works of Rothes, while distillery engineering is the business of such firms as Alexander Dey Ltd of Huntly, Hamilton Brothers of Buckie and Newmill Ironworks of Elgin. The firm of Speyside Cooperage Ltd of Craigellachie manufacture casks and also build the big fermentation vats or wash backs made out of Oregon pine and capable of holding 10,000 gallons of wash. Smaller cooperages deal with cask manufacture and some produce small tubs suitable for garden use. Clearly, therefore, the whisky business makes a major contribution to the economy of the Outer Regions, especially in Speyside where both distilling and related activities are numerous. With this importance, however, goes a danger. Not only is the industry unsatisfactory from a regional point of view in that it offers few highly paid jobs requiring valuable skills while the capital-intensive nature of the industry is leading to a run-down even among relatively unskilled jobs, but the lack of diversification in the Speyside area could be very serious if there was to be a recession in the industry. The situation has been closely studied by E. T. Parham who recently produced a report on the area for North-east Scotland Development Association (NESDA).[34]

'Scotch' accounts by value for rather more than 2 per cent of the country's exports and since World War II it has been the most consistent and often the largest dollar-earning export. And the rate of increase in exports cannot be equalled by any other major industry. Does the industry face any real threat? The outlook gives rise to confidence, but certain character-istics of the industry cannot be viewed with complete equanimity. First, although Scotch has a unique reputation with a legal definition which includes distillation in Scotland, it is, as M. C. Storrie pointed out, in her geographical review of the industry 'a luxury product liable to fluctuations of taste and demand'.[35] The industry remains nervous that Japan may one day become a major producer and exporter of whisky.[36] At present the demand comes overwhelmingly from abroad, accounting for 84.7 per cent of the total sales of 81.3 million gallons in 1972 (79.2 per cent of a total sale of 38 million gallons in 1962). Over the period foreign sales have increased by 129 per cent (home sales by 58 per cent). The pattern of export is laid out in Fig 12, and this brings out the prime importance of the American market. How far can present trends be projected into the future? The industry must plan years in advance and expansion undertaken at present anticipates further rises in demand over the next decade. Not only is capital committed in buildings and plant, but huge whisky stocks are accumulating: 957.4 million gallons in March 1973, more than ten times the total sales in that year. As a ratio of annual sales the stocks have not increased over the last decade, but the huge investment locked up in bonded warehouses is a source of some misgiving in the industry and some feel that it would be prudent to show more restraint and stop producing nearly twice the amount that is actually sold.

A second theme concerns the control of the distilleries. Because of the growth of the blending companies in Central Scotland, control has long since moved away from the Highland area in the majority of cases. But 'a large and increasing section of the industry is now owned by English and overseas concerns greedy for the profit to be made from the continuing boom in the worldwide consumption of Scotch'.[37] In fact, some 40 per cent of marketing companies have head offices outside Scotland, and 15 per cent outside the UK. The special advantages of American subsidiaries in entering the USA market

gives them a particularly strong position, and they have been
present in Scotland since the end of Prohibition. The foreign-
based blenders are also extending backwards into distilling,
following the lead of the Scottish blenders. Hiram Walker, the
Canadian firm, acquired Glenburgie distillery near Elgin in
1930 and has subsequently extended to five other Highland malt
distilleries and a Lowland malt and grain complex at Dumbarton.
In addition there are the blending and bottling plants owned
by this company. Among the American firms, Schenley Industries
may be cited. They acquired Long John International in 1956
Blending operations for Long John extended back into distilling,
notably through control of Kinclaith (Glasgow) Lowland malt
and grain complex and the malt distilleries of Laphroaig
(Islay), Glenugie and Tormore. Whatever policitcal progress
Scotland's drive for devolution may make with the aid of the
economic weight of whisky (and the black black oil), it seems
only too likely that national control of the industry will
diminish.

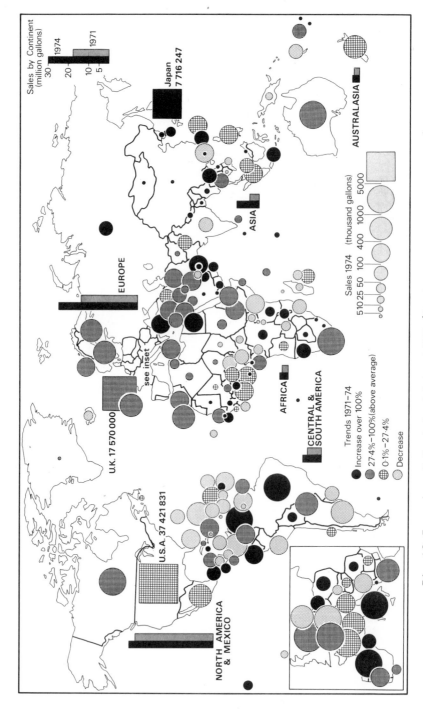

Fig 12 Exports of Scotch whisky 1973 (Scotch Whisky Association)

4

Some Further Industrial Studies

This chapter deals with four industrial sectors and builds on
the general employment patterns sketched in Chapter 1. For
each industry a brief summary is attempted, followed by
examination in depth of one significant case example.

Metallurgy

Despite considerable optimism expressed in the pages of
early nineteenth-century gazetteers, the mining of metalliferous
minerals has never achieved any great importance. An early iron
industry on the shores of Loch Marree was supported by local
ore and charcoal, while ferrous minerals have been found in
Raasay (Skye & Lochalsh) Tomintoul (Moray) and Sandlodge
(Shetland), the magnetite in the latter location being worked
for some years after World War II. Non-ferrous ores have
attracted more sustained interest. Included here are the
antimony of Glendinning (Annandale & Eskdale) , lead at
Strontian (Lochaber) and Wanlockhead (Nithsdale), silver, mined
along with lead, in Islay (Argyll), not to mention the western-
style 'gold rush' to Kildonan (Sutherland). But apart from
Wanlockhead, exploitation tended to be spasmodic,[1] illustrated
by the experience of copper mining at Sandlodge (Shetland):
exploitation extended from the late eighteenth-century shaft
sinking by Welsh miners to the extensions of 1907 which
revealed new pockets of both copper pyrites and iron ore
(haematite), but production never extended beyond a few shipments apart from the vigorous efforts from 1874 to 1881 which
followed the installation of crushing and washing apparatus.[2]
In the Highlands grants and loans have been made available to
mining companies and the HIDB have commissioned mineral
assessments, but there is no prospect so far that any
metalliferous minerals will be exploited as a result. Nevertheless, metallurgical industries have been established in the

Outer Regions. In the eighteenth century, Highland charcoal resources attracted iron smelting using English ores, and these ventures survived until c. 1820 and c. 1870 in the cases of Furnace (Loch Fyne) and Bonawe respectively, despite the introduction of coke smelting at Carron in the Central Belt in 1760.[3] Today Scotland's iron and steel industry uses foreign ores and although no plant has yet been built at a tidewater site, the Central Belt will almost certainly continue to exert a monopoly as present interest in the Hunterston (Strathclyde) site indicates.[4] One other important example concerns the production of aluminium. The Highlands contain all Scotland's reduction plant (for the conversion of alumina, aluminium oxide, to aluminium), and this activity is significant enough to warrant fuller consideration in the rest of this section.

Aluminium was first produced by reducing aluminium chloride vapour with potassium, a process developed by H. Wöhler at Göttingen in Germany in 1845, following earlier experiments by H. C. Oersted in 1824 and H. Davy in 1809. The method was perfected in France by S. C. Deville in 1854, and the interest by Napoleon III in the possible military applications of aluminium helped to stimulate interest. But the cost was excessive, and even though there was a fall to £3,000 per ton in 1889 compared with the equivalent of £50,000 in Deville's time, the metal was still only suitable for luxury use. Yet seven years later aluminium was selling for only £163 per ton. This was due to new processes. First a new method of producing alumina from bauxite was discovered by K. J. Bayer in Austria between 1887 and 1892, and secondly an electrolytic reduction process was developed independently by C. M. Hall in the USA and P. L. T. Heroult in France. Alumina was made to dissolve with the use of cryolite as a flux. Available in commercial quantities only in Greenland, cryolite proved an excellent catalyst for it was lighter than aluminium, which sank to the bottom of the cell to be drawn off periodically without interrupting a continuous process.

By 1893 the Hall – Heroult process was untried in business but users of the Deville method included two firms from the English Midlands: Websters Aluminium Crown Metal Company at Solihull and the Aluminium Company at Oldbury, set up in 1882 and 1887 respectively (Bell Brothers at Washington in Durham also operated the process between 1860 and 1872). As employed today, 1 ton of aluminium requires double the quantity of alumina, plus 1–2cwt of cryolite, 10–11cwt of carbon and 17,500–19,000Kwh of electricity.[5] The 2 ton of alumina in turn requires double the weight of bauxite together with 3cwt

of caustic soda and the heat equivalent of 2 tons of coal.
Clearly, the electricity consumption is an important element in
total production costs, up to 20 per cent. Therefore, the
supply must not only be continuous but relatively cheap. For
many years hydroelectricity has been the cheapest source,
provided the power was used at source and provided that
physical conditions would be found where the required output
could be obtained without excessively elaborate waterworks.
Scotland's initial interest in aluminium reduction stemmed
from the Highland water-power potential which in the early
years was large enough to support efficient reduction works.

The North British Aluminium Company set up in 1894 to use
the Bayer and Hall – Heroult processes in Britain.[6] Guided by
Lord Kelvin, pioneer of electricity, as scientific advisor, the
company commenced operations in 1895 at the Falls of Foyers
(Inverness). Although the catchment area was quite large, the
head was rather limited (Table 7). Yet at a time when technology
was limited (the down take pipes were made of cast iron and
not capable of standing very high water pressures) and world
demand for aluminium as low as 2,000 ton per annum, the scheme
represented the optimum scale of working. Until maximum output
of 1,000 per annum was reached (after 1904), as much as 80 per
cent of the power was used for experimentation and for calcium-
carbide production. Rising world demand called for further
exploitation of water rights which the company had secured in
1894, but a large scale of activity was now warranted, and the
vital statistics of the Kinlochleven plant opened in 1909 are
of a totally different order to those of the Foyers factory.
At the time, however, the company appreciated the limited
capacity of Highland water catchments, and from 1907 began to
invest in Norway. Ingots are still supplied from Eydehaven and
Tyssedal, and super-purity aluminium is supplied from Vikeland,
converted in 1946. It seems likely that further development in
Scotland was stimulated in part by strategic considerations,
as well as the tremendous growth in popularity of the metal as
a result of its extensive use during World War I. A minor
extension to the Kinlochleven catchment area was made by
linkage with the small reservoir of Loch Eilde Mor, but more
ambitious proposals of 1918 for the supply of water from Loch
Treig were opposed by Inverness County Council who were anxious
that the water should be used for industrial development in the
Fort William area and not at Kinlochleven where the factory
was situated in Argyll. With further pressure from Lochaber
Development Association, the company's proposals of 1919
envisaged a tunnel to take Loch Treig water to a new Lochaber
factory. Completion of the tunnel in 1929 meant the opening of

Table 7

BRITISH ALUMINIUM COMPANY: HIGHLAND REDUCTION WORKS

Works	Building	Head (m)	Catchment (sq km)	Power Supply Capacity (MW)	Grid Supply (MW)	Reservoirs (million galls)	Furnaces Number	Amps 000s	Production 1943 (000 tons)	Production 1973 (000 tons)	1973 Employment
Foyers	1895-6	107	83[4]	3.64		Loch Mhor 575	na	8	1[7]		[9]
Kinlochleven	1904-9[1]	305	160	24.00	8.0[5]	Blackwater 3930	56	40[6]	7	11	350
Fort William	1924-43[2]	244	785	82.25	16.5[5]	Loch Treig 7370 Loch Laggan 1401	124	94	22[8]	26	500
Invergordon	1968-73[3]				200.0		320	130		100	750

1 Aluminium was first produced in a temporary works opened 1907; 2 opened in three stages, completed in 1929, 1933 and 1943; 3 jetty and carbon factory opened 1970 and first cell (furnace) line 1971; 4 additional 176sq km of the catchment area of the Foyers river is included; 5 negotiated with NSHEB in 1966. Smaller capacities of 6.0 and 8.5mw negotiated in 1961; 6 experiments ranged upwards from 16,000 amps; 7 initially 200 tons. Before closure in 1967 annual production was 600 tons of super-purity metal; 8 national output was increased by a works at Dolgarrog opened in 1908 and by wartime emergency capacity at Rheola and Port Tennant, using methods which would have been uneconomic in peacetime. Even so total reduction capacity of 55,000 ton fell far short of fabrication capacity of 270,000 tons; 9 80 employed when works closed

Source: BAC

the first phase of the scheme. It was followed by a second
phase in 1933, when the water from an enlarged Loch Laggan was
fed into Loch Treig, and a third phase opened ten years later
when water from Upper Spey was ponded back by a weir and fed
into Loch Laggan. This elaborate linkage gave a very large
catchment area, but it was significant that the whole scheme
was launched with the help of a government guarantee covering
the issue of debentures, and the final phase was implemented
during World War II and completed with military assistance.
Even before the first phase of the scheme was complete, a 360mw
hydro station was supplying a reduction factory in Canada with
investment per unit of capacity less than half that required
in the Highlands.[7] Whereas the Highland reduction capacity
accounted for 10 per cent of world production in 1896 (2.0
thousand tons) and 6 per cent in 1919 (0.13 million tons), the
proportion fell to barely a third of 1 per cent in 1970 (10.24).

It seemed that the Lochaber works would mark the end of an
unprecedented half-century of heavy industrial development in
the Highlands. However, even in the limited context of aluminium
reduction this forecast has been invalidated. The increasing
efficiency of steam-powered stations and the scope for special
arrangements with power suppliers, led to investigations by
the major aluminium companies, including BAC, during the 1960s.
Political support was added in 1967 because new reduction works
were seen as one means of introducing new industries to
development areas and reducing the disparity between reduction
capacity of 35,000 ton and fabricating capacity ten times that
figure.[8] Firms were invited to submit plant with a view to
the establishment of two works, each with 120,000 ton capacity.
In view of the need to import either bauxite or alumina, a
port in the development areas, close to the grid, would be an
appropriate location. In this context the interest in the
Cromarty Firth (Ross & Cromarty) by both Alcan and BAC may be
appreciated, although it is not clear how crucial was the
encouragement and promotion by the HIDB with whom both
companies had made contacts by 1967. Alcan eventually settled
for an English location, and BAC announced their plans for
Invergordon in 1968. They had considered more than twenty
other locations, and would have settled for either one other
Scottish site (Hunterston) or three sites elsewhere in the UK:
Blyth, Seaton Carew and Milford Haven. However, it was only at
Invergordon that all the desirable needs were satisfied.
These include flat land close to a sheltered deep-water harbour,
plentiful supply of process water (3 million gallons per day
is used at the factory), convenience for linkage with the grid
and the rail system (with transport to Falkirk rolling mill
especially important), local labour availability and easy

liaison with the other Highland reduction works.[9] There was the problem of insufficiently firm ground, and the construction on Inverbreakie Farm had to be piled due to the high load-bearing factor; but most other locations would have been unsatisfactory to some degree on this point.

Drawing all its power from the grid, the Invergordon factory is extremely vulnerable to power cuts. Despite connection to 132kv as well as 275kv lines, grid failure has been experienced, leading to widespread rupturing of electrodes. Advance warning of power cuts avoids damage but means a serious loss of efficiency. On the whole, however, the Invergordon plant is a highly competitive unit and must pose questions for the survival of the older factories. The Foyers works, converted in 1954 to the production of super-purity aluminium (appreciated for its extreme ductility and high resistance to corrosion, hence used in cable sheathing, car trim, light reflectors and roof covering), was closed in 1967 and now stands empty. But when Invergordon was first publicly mooted, BAC considered that Fort William and Kinlochleven were thoroughly viable operations in their own right. Both should continue in operation with many years of useful life ahead provided they continue to be operated efficiently. Efficiency has been improved by use of power from the grid when water is in short supply during drought or when demand for metal justifies the use of relatively expensive power; and there has also been a substantial reduction in the workforce, especially at Kinlochleven. Although Invergordon has increased its payroll beyond the planned 'flat total' of 550, its high level of automation gives a marked contrast with the older works when output is related to employment.

In all cases the reduction works have made a big impact on their respective areas. Even at Foyers the intrusion of industry into a rural area caused local resentment, but all the factories have won a considerable measure of local acceptance, including Invergordon where the use of good agricultural land inflamed the opposition of an influential minority. The employment has, of course, been highly appreciated ever since the Foyers proposal inspired 'a genuine hope that the devastating tide of emigration may be stayed'.[10] But the task of the company extends from factory operation to community development. At Foyers the Old Foyers House had to be restored for use as a temporary hostel while the houses for a community of 600 people were being built. At Kinlochleven there was again little existing settlement and the company had to follow the example of guests to Mamore Lodge and use water transport. The loch had to be dredged and a pier built before construction work on the factory itself could begin.

Not until 1927 was the road connection completed right round the head of the loch and until that time the Loch Leven Shipping Company served the needs of the village. Well might a company brochure claim that the development had 'caused a stir in the western Highlands comparable to a minor gold rush'.[11] But the village built by the company through the Kinlochleven Village Improvement Society, with a population exceeding 1,200 by 1910, has always suffered from its unfortunate aspect, the southern half cut off by high ground from any direct winter sunshine. Extension of development northwards across the river has meant an administrative divide since the river forms the county boundary, although amenities have improved as a result. Economically the village is tied very closely to the factory, and the absence of diversification has made it vulnerable to a rundown in employment from some 500 before World War II to approximately 350 today. Had better communications been available at the time of construction, the existing settlements nearer the mouth of Loch Leven might well have been a more desirable location for the industrial community. At both Fort William and Invergordon the aluminium factories have been grafted on to substantial communities.[12] At Fort William the company provided housing through the Inverlochy Village Improvement Society, but as at Kinlochleven there is a growing local authority involvement and this has been predominant from the outset at Invergordon.[13] Also illustrative of the different situation is the company's involvement in community projects: a recreation centre was provided at Kinlochleven in 1970 following a similar move at Fort William, but at Invergordon the company has tried to integrate into the community without undue paternalism and seeks to encourage development of facilities without wholesale sponsoring which may lead to discrimination, as at Fort William. One other interesting consequence of the BAC presence in the Highlands has been the development of estates embracing the catchment areas. Land ownership was sought in some cases in order to avoid high claims for compensation as a result of waterworks, but at Kinlochleven the purchase of Mamore estate was necessary in order to obtain ground for housing across the county boundary. The land acquisitions were thus incidental to the aluminium projects and resulted from local circumstances. However, the company endeavours to make the best use of the land commensurate with economic circumstances. Hill sheep farming is organised by a number of tenants, and a useful crop of venison is also obtained. A substantial forestry programme has been implemented since World War II.

The final question concerns the functional relationships between the reduction works and other stages of production. Foyers was initially linked by sea transport (using the Caledonian Canal) with the Larne alumina works (processing the Antrim bauxite) and the Greenock carbon factory, and a roughly circular supply pattern was completed by delivery of chemicals to Larne from Runcorn on the Mersey where the aluminium ingots were offloaded. The metal was delivered from there to premises at Milton (Staffordshire) acquired in 1895 from the Cowles Syndicate who had set up in 1888 to produce aluminium alloys from French aluminium by electro-thermal processes.[14] Casting of alloys was eventually superseded by rolling sheet and strip and production of rods, wire and rivets. A small foundry and rolling mill operated at Greenock from 1895 to 1903. Kinlochleven was then plugged into this water-transport system, but the carbon factory at Kinlochleven cut out the need for the Greenock plant (closed 1909), and the expansion of finishing at Milton (where an extrusion press was installed in 1911) was followed by the acquisition of further premises near the Ship Canal at Warrington for sheet and strip production in 1912 (Fig 13). The transport system became more diverse after World War I. The Larne alumina plant (now processing French bauxite) was supplemented by the Burntisland factory in 1917. This factory could supply Foyers by boat via Inverness, but rail transport could serve the Lochaber plant and after World War II, when Larne factory closed, rail transport was used for Kinlochleven, with transfer to road vehicles at the railhead of Ballachulish (Fort William in 1966). The emergency of World War II brought temporary reduction capacity to Wales, extensions to the rolling mills including a new mill at Falkirk (to supply aircraft works in Scotland and Northern England), and a refinery for aluminium scrap at Latchford near Warrington.[15] This affected the postwar dispatch of ingots from the reduction works since Falkirk was now the main destination, with some of the metals moved by road tanker. At present the situation is highly complex: all three main transport forms are used, although this varies according to the material and the factory situation. Invergordon now receives alumina from the Caribbean works of Reynolds Metals Co, delivered at the new jetty by ships of some 30,000 ton. Alumina is distributed to Fort William by rail (via Glasgow!) but to Kinlochleven by road. Pitch is supplied to all three factories by road, but petroleum coke (for anode blocks) goes to Fort William by rail from Grangemouth with distribution by road to Invergordon and Kinlochleven. Anthracite (for cathode lining material) is delivered to Kinlochleven by sea (the only use of sea transport there now); it is calcined at Kinlochleven for distribution to the other two smelters by

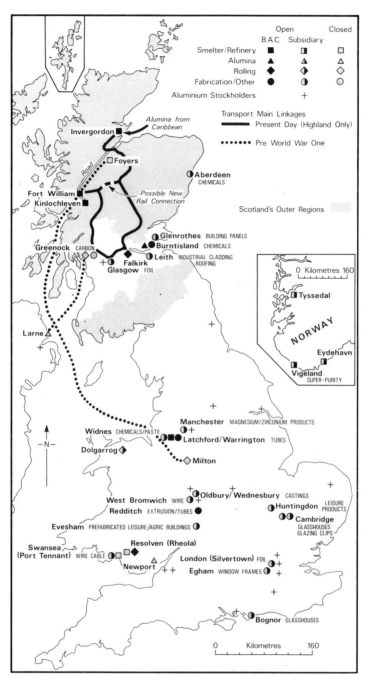

Open   Closed
B.A.C. Subsidiary

Smelter/Refinery   ■   ◧   □
Alumina   ▲   △   △
Rolling   ◆   ◈   ◇
Fabrication/Other   ●   ◑   ○

Aluminium Stockholders   +

Transport Main Linkages
━━━━━   Present Day (Highland Only)
●●●●●   Pre World War One

Invergordon   Alumina from Caribbean

Road   Foyers

Fort William   Aberdeen CHEMICALS
Kinlochleven   Possible New Rail Connection

Scotland's Outer Regions

0   Kilometres   160

Greenock CARBON   Glenrothes BUILDING PANELS
Burntisland CHEMICALS
Falkirk   Leith INDUSTRIAL CLADDING ROOFING
Glasgow FOIL

Tyssedal

NORWAY

Eydehavn
Vigeland SUPER-PURITY

Larne

Manchester MAGNESIUM/ZIRCONIUM PRODUCTS
Widnes CHEMICALS/PASTE
—N—   Latchford/Warrington TUBES
Dolgarrog   Milton

West Bromwich WIRE   Oldbury/Wednesbury CASTINGS
Redditch EXTRUSION/TUBES   Huntingdon LEISURE PRODUCTS
Cambridge GLASSHOUSES GLAZING CLIPS
Evesham PREFABRICATED LEISURE/AGRIC BUILDINGS

Swansea   Resolven (Rheola)
(Port Tennant) WIRE CABLE   London (Silvertown) FOIL
Newport   Egham WINDOW FRAMES

Bognor GLASSHOUSES

0   Kilometres   160

Fig 13 British Aluminium installations (BAC)

road. Cryolite is brought in by sea to Inverness for distribution to the smelters, again by road, but this is not necessary
for Invergordon where the cryolite is constantly recycled. The
ingots, rolling slabs, extrusion billets and wire bars are sent
south by road or rail, but Invergordon also has some direct
export overseas. Falkirk remains the principal rolling plant,
but the smaller units survive, apart from Milton which closed
in 1965. Burntisland alumina plant, using Ghanaian bauxite, is
retained for special alumina used for various chemical processes,
including conversion to aluminium sulphate required in paper
manufacture and water purification. Company policy was formerly
to concentrate on semi-finished articles, but the world surplus
in reduction capacity very evident in 1970 and 1971 (which
delayed full capacity working at Invergordon) led to greater
interest in aluminium-using industries producing cable, foil
and wire as well as castings, chemicals, glasshouses, leisure
products and window frames. Such units are now included in a
growing number of subsidiary companies.

Engineering

There is a significant growth of light engineering and
repair facilities throughout the Outer Regions, and important
local manufactures have generated their own suppliers. Thus
the Borders textile industry stimulated the local development
of textile machinery, and the distilleries of the Moray District
are supported by engineering firms in Dufftown, Elgin, Huntly
and Rothes. In both cases there has been some expansion into
other fields: at Annan boilermaking was established in 1898,
and in 1947 another unit was started for production of cranes
and waggon tipplers - and in Elgin engineering for the oil
industry has been an important recent development. But the
highly complex engineering sector is best represented in
Aberdeen and Dundee. In these two cities particularly strong
demand arises for machinery and equipment for indigenous
industries and activities. In Aberdeen the granite industry
created a demand for cutting and polishing equipment produced
by George Cassie & Sons and Alexander Wilson, not to mention
the Bon Accord Pneumatic Tools of Wilmar Engineering. The
paper industry is served by Bell & Robertson, specialising in
papermaking machinery. The food industry draws fish-gutting
machines from C. F. Wilson & Co (1932), and insulated/refridg-
erated containers from the recently established firm of Body
Engineering. William MacKinnon, with a long experience in
general engineering dating back to 1789, export equipment for
the cocoa, coffee, sugar and rice industries, illustrating the
scope for firms initially dependent on the local market to

find market outlets, despite distance from the main sources of metal, given high levels of quality and specialisation. Lifting gear for public works produced since 1866 by J. M. Henderson also goes largely for export. In Dundee and the Tayside region engineering and electrical goods manufacture is expected to replace textiles as the most important manufacturing group during the 1970s.[16]

In both cities fabrication is evident in the production of agricultural machinery, produced in Aberdeen by Allan Brothers and R. G. Garvie & Sons. This activity has spread through the Grampian region, including small communities such as Fetterangus, Rothienorman and Udny as well as the former burghs of Ellon, Huntly, Inverurie, Keith and Turriff. At Rothienorman the firm of Fraser Brothers dates back to 1946 when the village smithy was taken over. The premises have been substantially enlarged and the output of bruisers, buckrakes, forklifts and trailers is sold in various parts of the UK and also abroad. The work-force of approximately fifty is not drawn entirely from the village, for commuting extends into the Aberchirder, Forgue and Fyvie areas. Gray's of Fetterangus, founded in 1927, have enjoyed similar success, emphasising 'the vital role of enterprise in the conduct of business'.[17] Inverurie has a substantially larger industry based on the decision of the Great North of Scotland Railway to establish their railway workshops in the town in 1902. The premises were closed in 1969 but purchased by Aberdeen County Council and subsequently passed to new users: Cruickshank & Partners, electrical engineers, who moved from Kirkintilloch and the Inverurie Boiler & Engineering Works (a subsidiary of the Motherwell firm Marshall Anderson). Another incoming firm is Ross & Bonnyman (Engineering), producing roller pallets and other distribution and handling equipment, who were attracted from Renfrew on account of the engineering tradition in Inverurie.

However, the spread of light engineering is now quite considerable throughout the Outer Regions although most evident in towns with good communications, labour catchments and technical-training facilities. Elgin's new industries include the telecommunication instruments of Caledonian Microwave while Fraserburgh, the location of the Buchan Technical College, has added Doig Springs (Scotland) to its older toolmaking and fabrication industries, and Inverness has attracted machine-tool manufacture by AI Welders, electric alternators production by Markon Engineering and electronics by Precision Relays. Other towns have also benefitted, notably Buckie where the bulb factory of Thorn Lighting Company, started in 1956, now employs

350 and Campbeltown where the range of industries includes
aero-engine components, heating and ventilating equipment,
precision parts of machinery for the synthetic fibre industry,
and writing utensils. Even small branch factories in remote
areas have flourished. The trend began with Rollo Industries
establishing small workshops at Kinloch Rannoch (Perth &
Kinross) and Inverasdale (Ross & Cromarty) to produce components
for the mother factory in Bonnybridge. But other examples now
include the supply of components for the thermostats of Tarka
Controls (Inverness) from Barra and manufacture of parts by
Sykes Robertson (Electronics) at Sanday, Orkney. According to
P. Bailey this latter firm prospers 'not because of any
advantage of location in Sanday but because of the international
reputation of its founder as a technical expert and inventor
and because it exploits markets left in the electronics business
by the major companies'.[18] And at local level the survival of
the village smithy may be noted, sometimes with diversification
extending to general engineering and steel erection.

Of special interest because of its historic significance,
its current dynamism and its relevance to most parts of the
Outer Regions is boatbuilding and marine engineering (Fig 14b).
The industry is heavily concentrated in the Central Belt, but
it is interesting to recall that early experiments in steam
navigation took place in 1788 on Loch Dalswinton (Nithsdale)
when P. Miller and others put their 'double pleasure boat' on
trial. However, the building of steamships extended to Dundee
where the Dundee Foundry, a pioneer of heavy engineering and
machinemaking, was acquired by the Gourlay family in 1846 and
geared to shipbuilding from 1854. Earlier pioneer firms in the
building of iron ships had failed, but the pool of skilled
labour was recruited by Gourlays, turning out ships for the
coasting trade and expanding to larger vessels for oceanic
trading after the move from Marine Parade to more extensive
premises at Camperdown in 1870. By 1900 ships of up to 5,000
ton were being built, but unfortunately the decision to re-equip,
taken in 1905, was followed by a lean period and the company
was liquidated in 1910. Whalers were built in the late nineteenth century in the 'Arctic Yard' of Alexander Stephen. The
shipbuilding industry survives in Dundee today through the
Caledon yard of the Robb Caledon Group building such specialised
vessels as ferries, newsprint carriers and sludge tankers.

At Aberdeen, shipbuilding developed from the middle of the
eighteenth century and by the early nineteenth century its
tonnage of sailing ships exceeded that of any other Scottish
port. The firm of Alexander Hall & Company was founded in 1790

and built many of the famous tea clippers, such as <u>Cairngorm</u> and <u>Thermopylae</u>, introduced on the China run after 1850. Such voyages ended in 1878 after years of competition with steamships using the Suez route, but the Aberdeen yards were able to specialise in building steam trawlers for the city's rapidly expanding fishing industry. Although this business is still important, with substantial foreign orders (notably stern trawlers and factory/refridgerated vessels), other types of vessel have been built beginning with dredgers and tugs in the 1920s. In recent years the output has included cargo ships (including heavy-lift vessels and a sulphuric-acid carrier), car ferries and fishery research vessels, while one company has announced its intention of building oil-rig supply vessels.[19]

Smaller yards in the Grampian and Highland regions have close links with the fishing industry. An important business continues to be the production of wooden fishing vessels. Motor boats were introduced from 1906, but current designs still show some affinity with the sailing boats which culminated in the decked <u>Zulu</u> introduced at Lossiemouth in 1879. By incorporating the projecting stern of the <u>Scaffie</u> with the vertical stem of the <u>Fifie</u>, tonnage remained unchanged but there was greater space on deck and greater ease of handling. Most of the Grampian yards, with up to fifty employees, are able to build boats of up to 80ft in length suitable for both seine netting or pair trawling. Homegrown oak and larch is used and boats are constructed according to the yard's individual design and owner's specification. Some yards concentrate their workforce on one vessel while others may have several boats at different stages of completion.

The Macduff Boatbuilding Company have a large shed enabling one boat to be started under cover while another is on the slipway. The larger Buckie firm of Herd & Mackenzie has more extensive accommodation and a wider product range. In addition to fishing boats (built of steel as well as wood), luxury 'Spay' class yachts are built and the yard recently completed the <u>Captain Scott</u>, an adventure training schooner now based at Plockton with the Loch Eil Trust. With a length of 144ft this was the largest wooden sailing ship built in Britain since the turn of the century. Several other yards have their specialities outside the fishing industry: Arbuthnott's at Montrose build lifeboats as well as salmon cobles, while Noble's at Fraserburgh build car ferries in addition to their work for the local fleet. Ship repairs and fitting out, including defouling and painting, also constitute important business, and Herd & Mackenzie at Buckie specialise in lifeboat repair. Marine and structural

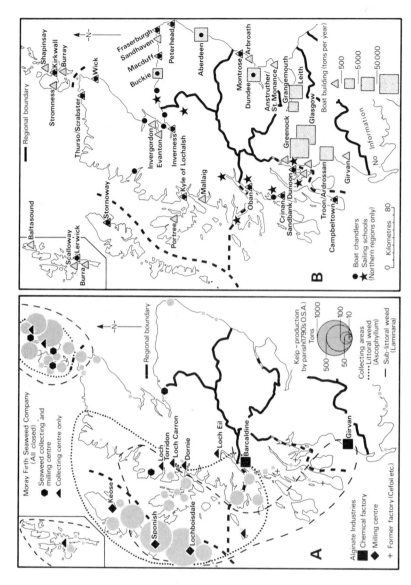

Fig 14. A: seaweed processing; B: boat building
(Various sources see notes 20, 22, 29, 31)

engineering, allied with the boatbuilding industry, has achieved some importance at the main Grampian ports including Peterhead, Fraserburgh, Macduff, Buckie and Lossiemouth. These yards are highly specialised: propeller repairs at Buckie and winch manufacture at Lossiemouth. It is possible that the tradition has been a marginal factor in the establishment of larger engineering firms, such as Consolidated Pneumatic Tool Company at Fraserburgh in 1904 (extended to converted war-industry premises in Aberdeen in 1947) and Cleveland Twist Drill at Peterhead in 1957.

In the Highlands the industry operates at a rather smaller scale, and until recently was in a somewhat moribund state with only limited capacity and small local demand For example, in Argyll & Bute, which seems to offer ideal bases for ship building and repair, the number of yards is very small. But the recent revival of Highland fishing has provided an opportunity for the HIDB to develop boatbuilding. A number of yards can only handle small craft. Small boats suitable for shell fishing, sea angling and livestock ferrying in the islands are turned out by the Invergordon Boatyard and Currie's of Portbeag, Oban, using the traditional clinker construction At Tarbert the old yard of Dickie's has seen some revival with construction of cabin cruisers and the fitting out of small steel boats, importing hulls from England, while cutters and yachts form the core of the business at the Sandbank yard of Alex Robertson & Sons. But the revival of the industry has been accompanied by introduction of new boatbuilding materials. The Campbeltown Shipyard, closed in 1922 after forty-five years work, was reopened in 1969 as a Lithgow subsidiary to build all-steel boats. Building up from repair functions, the first purpose-built trawler was launched in 1970 This was a 50ft vessel, but since then great interest has attached to a 80ft vessel (for seining or pair trawling) and many 36ft boats (for shell fishing, scallop dredging and sea angling) have been completed.

A second innovation has been the use of glass-reinforced plastic for hulls, following proven wooden designs. The Havant-based firm of Halmatic came to former aircraft premises at Hatston, Kirkwall following appreciation of local-market possibilities through a holiday in the area by a company director. Production moulds should eventually range from 36ft to 75ft, turning out standard hulls which can then be fitted out by existing Orkney builders. The first was completed in 1972 at the yard of James Duncan at Burray, but Stromness yards may also be interested, including the firm of J. T.

Anderson which has combined ideas from several countries to produce a standard transom-sterned boat of 21ft fitted out for either lobster fishing, sea angling or family cruising. Finally, ferrocement has been pioneered at the Scrabster Boat-yard near Thurso (as well as Lossiemouth). This specialised form of reinforced concrete involves many layers of thinly divided steel reinforcement and special mortar. A hull of less than 1in in thickness has great strength and resilience; over a length of 50ft the vessel is probably lighter than the timber equivalent and certainly has more space due to the absence of heavy timber ribs and frames. However, the new materials offer the greatest advantage with the standard hull: none of them can match the versatility of wood which can easily be used to match the requirements of the individual owner.[20]

Chemicals

There are important ICI interests in the Aberdeen and Dumfries areas. A subsidiary, Scottish Agricultural Industries (formed in 1928), took over the chemical works at Sandilands, near Aberdeen harbour. It was built more than a century ago to dispose of residual products from the gasworks and manufacture fertiliser: ammonium sulphate, bone meal and fish meal (superphosphate later). An important expansion came in 1953 with the new sulphuric-acid plant and extension of production to superphosphate turned out as a granular compound fertiliser at Dyce, where chemical plant built in 1869 and extended in 1946 is integrated with the initial Sandilands installation. In Dumfries the chemical industry dates to the strategic develop-ment by the Ministry of Supply at Drungans in 1939 for gun cotton and Powfoot in 1949 for nitro-cellulose powders and high explosives. Both plants continue in operation, Drungans for cellulose derivatives and polyester/polypropylene film for recording tape and packaging (this followed abortive attempts to develop a protein-fibre plant between 1952 and 1957), and Powfoot with the continuing interest in military requirements supplemented by products for the paint and leather industries. Since World War II, Dumfries has been selected by an Edinburgh firm for a branch factory producing rubber boots and casual footwear, while Michelin have divided the stages of tyre production between new plants at Aberdeen and Perth.

Smaller innovations include the manufacture of quality glassware at Oban and Wick and the production of ink at Campbeltown. Other recently established activities include manufacture of polyester resin castings at Evanton (Ross & Cromarty) by Shattaline, and various plastic extrusions at

108

Stonehaven by Albyn Plastics. However, the most persistent
theme in the chemical industry relates to the processing of
brown seaweed, either Laminaria drawn from the sub-littoral
region (below low water) or Ascophyllum from the littoral zone
within the tidal range. Seaweed is most common in Skye, the
Western Isles, the west mainland coasts of Lochaber, Ross &
Cromarty and in Orkney and Shetland.[21] It is believed that
dense growth is only possible in areas subjected to moderate
wave action by enriched ocean water, hence the comparatively
scanty growth in both the very exposed western waters and the
relatively quiet inshore waters of the east coast. The modern
industry was preceded by a much older activity concerned with
the extraction of vegetable alkali from seaweed ash, while it
should not be overlooked that in the past, and still at the
present time in some localities, the use of seaweed for
fertilising agricultural land has been appreciated. Of course,
it was only certain coastal districts which could receive a
dressing of seaweed and the literature records how, for example,
distance from the sea was a serious constraint on the
improvement of the interior of the Orkney islands in the late
eighteenth century.[22]

    Areas blessed by an abundance of seaweed were also able
to indulge in the production of kelp, the name usually applied
to calcined seaweed ash, although at times it attaches to the
seaweed in its natural state. Since the alkali contained in
the ash was valuable in soap and glass production, it was
reasonable to expect that the early Scottish chemical industry
might make extensive use of domestic seaweed resources. Indeed,
the first reference to the kelp industry dates to the late
seventeenth century.[23] But since Scottish kelp was not then
competitive, the main alkali demand was met by imports of
barilla from the Mediterranean and of wood-ash from the Baltic
and North America. However, duties levied on imports stimulated
the domestic industry so that the early eighteenth century is
marked by a diffusion of the industry from North Uist to the
rest of the Hebrides and also to parts of the mainland,
especially the section from Loch Carron to Loch Broom, areas
characterised by a seasonal burst of activity in cutting,
drying and processing. In Orkney the kelp was crucial in
paying high farm rents since markets for agricultural products
were very poor.[24] Quality was particularly good, and the
product was much appreciated by Newcastle glassmakers, while
the resources were prolific enough to justify annual cutting.[25]
The industry reached boom proportions during the Napoleonic
Wars when all foreign supplies were cut off. While prices
always showed considerable annual fluctuation, the contrast

between prewar prices below £5 per ton and wartime levels in excess of £20 was quite exceptional.[26] The situation provided great opportunities for impecunious landlords to make high profits, although the insistence by the lairds over their property rights meant that farmers were denied valuable manure.

The buoyant kelp industry supported a relatively high density of population and allowed radical programmes of estate reorganisation to be shelved. Unfortunately, the boom conditions were short-lived and high profits proved much too temporary for wealth to find its way to development of the community at large. Moreover, the industry taught no useful skills of permanent value to the many families who were drafted in during short periods of fine summer weather. Instead people were diverted from agricultural work and many were economically stranded when prices collapsed in the 1820s and ruined what was, in fact, a high-cost industry by comparison not only with foreign competitors but also with domestic alkali production using salt as the raw material. The discovery of the Stassfurt salts dealt the Scottish kelp industry a heavy blow. The traditional seaweed industry quickly contracted, and although it remained the principal manufacture in parts of the Western Isles at mid-century the price hardly justified the effort and it was argued that both time and raw material would have been better bestowed on the land.[27] There was some resuscitation based on iodine production. Coal- and peat-burning retorts were introduced to Tiree in 1863, but this activity ran at very low level after the 1880s, with the discovery of iodates in Chile.

By the early twentieth century, however, new uses for seaweed had been found. These are concerned with the organic constituents of seaweed, including alginic acid.[28] The incorporation of milled and ground seaweed meal in animal feeds, a process pioneered in the USA, was attempted from the time of World War I.[29] Apparently, a factory was built at Luing to produce feedstuffs for sheep, cattle and poultry but this was burnt down. Further momentum came after 1948 from the Scottish Seaweed Research Association. Moray Firth Seaweed Company operated factories at Nairn, Gairloch and Orkney (Kirkwall and Sanday - later Orphir). With the exception of the Nairn factory which had to import seaweed from collecting centres in Lochaber (Loch Eil) and Ross and Cromarty (Dornie, Loch Carron and Loch Torridon), these installations were located close to raw materials (Fig 14a, see p106). However, output was very modest (the Gairloch factory being intended to give out-of-season employment to local salmon fishermen). From a peak of 2,000 ton in 1955, production dropped to only 400 ton in 1960 when the industry was restricted to the Orkney factories.[30] All activity had ceased by 1962. High costs made the Scottish industries less profitable than their Irish counterparts, while the decline of the seaweed-collecting tradition inhibited high standards of raw-material production. Seaweed used for fertiliser is now imported, mainly from the Irish Republic and Norway.

But also significant was the growing competition for seaweed from the alginate industry.[31] It was in 1881 that sodium alginate was discovered and found to be useful as a textile size, and early in the present century firms began to use the material in this industry. In 1934 Cefoil was started with factories in Argyll (Bellochantuy and Kilmelford) for the manufacture of transparent wrapping film. During World War II alginates were appreciated in the manufacture of fireproof fibres for camouflage material and, under direction from the Ministry of Supply, Cefoil extended their operations from the original Kintyre base to new factories set up in 1942 in more northerly parts of Argyll, at Barcaldine and Kames, and also across the Firth of Clyde at Girvan (Strathclyde). After the war the factories came under the management of Alginate Industries Ltd. The Kintyre factory closed while Kames was relegated to the role of storage depot, leaving the chemical work to be concentrated on Barcaldine and Girvan. These factories enjoy reasonable access to the industrial core of Scotland, although the full story of location selection requires examination of the special conditions prevailing during the war. Locations were chosen by the Ministry of Supply to give work in areas where there was greatest labour available. The factories are well away from the main seaweed resources.

In manufacture, dried milled seaweed is fed into a maturing tank with alkali and hot water to yield sodium alginate liquor which is duly separated from the spent pulp in a settling vat. This material may be allowed to react with calcium chloride to produce a fibrous pulp, calcium alginate, with specialised industrial applications in textiles, while further stages in production involve conversion in an acid bath to alginic acid and subsequent mixing with soda to form a sodium alginate dough, milled into small particles. Blending of various alginates produces a range of some 200 finished products with highly diverse and specialised use. These include the quick disintegration of tablets in water, protection of roots during transplanting in forest nurseries, stabilising foam on beer, dental impression powders and viscosity control on high-speed paper machines. But textile printing remains the backbone of the market. Production has risen from 5 ton per week in the 1930s to some 150 ton today. The high export performance,

regularly in excess of two-thirds of production, has earned the
company widespread acclaim, including the Queen's Award for
Industry in 1968 and 1973. The 200 jobs at the Barcaldine
factory give a very significant boost to the economy of the Oban
and Lorn area of Argyll.

Both factories are poorly situated in relation to the main
seaweed-collection areas. Consequently, to avoid transport of
wet seaweed over uneconomic distances, drying and milling
factories have been set up in the Western Isles. Some weed may
be dried locally, on 'tangle dykes' in Orkney for example, but
the high rainfall and danger of decomposition calls for a
speedy artificial method of processing. Small coastal vessels
are chartered to collect seaweed from the various cutting points,
delivery to the milling factories and then convey the milled
weed straight to the chemical factories: milled Ascophyllum
going to Girvan and Laminaria to Barcaldine. Expanding output
places more pressure on seaweed collectors, but the assured
demand brings useful ancillary income to hundreds of small
holders who operate on a self-employed basis, although with
some help from the company and the HIDB over the provision of
boats. In Lochaber, seaweed collection is a year-round occupation, handled by two cutters based on Loch Sunartside at
Acharacle and Carna Island. Cutting has been extended to the
neighbouring lochs of Aline and Moidart, working on the basis
of a three-year regeneration period. Hand-operated serrated
sickles and air-driven scythes are used for cutting littoral
weed exposed at low tide, and this is then towed and assembled
in 'floats' of 20-40 ton. The floats may either be beached or
held at anchor at a suitable storage point pending transfer by
special lifting gear to the factory boat at approximately
fortnightly intervals. Cutting by one collector may easily
reach 100 ton per month, but variable weather prevents steady
progress and the amount sold may be seriously reduced by storm
losses. Such factors greatly reduce the potential available to
the industry. All the economically exploitable weed resources
in Scotland are now being used but the annual harvest is only
approximately 30,000 ton (of wet weed), whereas the Scottish
Seaweed Research Organisation revealed resources of 0.25
million ton of Ascophyllum, littoral weed and 4 million ton
of Laminaria, sub-littoral weed, which on the basis of a four-
year regeneration period could sustain a massive harvest.[32]
Since the industry requires more than 100,000 ton per annum,
the bulk of the supply to both factories must be imported,
from Iceland, Ireland, Norway and South Africa. To safeguard
future expansion plans, further searches have been necessary
and these have revealed the potential of the Falkland Islands

where enough weed can be harvested in the Port Stanley area to allow a ten-fold growth in _world_ production. A fifty-year concession has been obtained and the milled weed from Port Stanley may be used in the Scottish industry after 1975. It is possible that more effective harvesting machinery could be developed and some methods of farming seaweed might be devised. For _Laminaria_, usually collected off the beaches after it has been blown ashore, experiments are being conducted to see if the weed can be harvested by divers. But there are difficulties in cutting from a very rocky and uneven surface close inshore (at depths of up to 5 fathoms) and in transporting the weed which sinks when cut and has an unusually high water content. Under such conditions, efficient operation demands low working costs and harvesting boats must be of comparatively shallow draught and suitably engined and rigged to give a high degree of manoeuverability. The traditional method of working manually with poles from small boats would be quite uneconomic, yet mechanical harvesting could only be employed in favourable weather and would not allow discrimination between the fronds and stipes, for only the latter, containing the highest percentage of alginic acid can be used. More expensive to collect and mill than _Ascophyllum_, there could never be any question of all the industry's demands being met by these means.[33]

Tourism

Travellers have no doubt found pleasure and stimulation in the Scottish countryside for some centuries, although we know little of their early experiences.[34] But by the late eighteenth and early nineteenth centuries visitors were more able to publish their observations and these have become valuable research sources. The curative properties of mineral waters were appreciated: people afflicted with gout and rheumatism drank from the wells of Pannanich near Ballater (Kincardine & Deeside), while the water at the Hartfell Spa near Moffat (Annandale & Eskdale) was 'a powerful tonic and used for diseases of weakness'.[35] The period also witnesses a growing sensitivity by an exclusive group of upper-class travellers towards the physical landscape. Whereas the wild and barren mountain country had previously seemed uninviting, perhaps because the lowland mind had associated it with cultural backwardness, the wilderness, lying beyond the frontier of the improvements, was now to be embraced as an integral part of the national heritage. The period of romantic recreation, fostered by Sir Walter Scott and symbolised by the glamour of homespun cloth, stimulated a particularly strong attraction to deer stalking. The traditional pastime of the deer hunt became more institutionalised after the improving movement, with deer forests restricted to the mountain cores and fenced off from surrounding farmlands.[36] Outside interest was limited at first, although the Duke of Bedford came North for the season as early as 1818.

It was Queen Victoria's visit to Atholl in 1844 and the experiences of W. Scrope, stalking on that estate in Glenbruar, which fostered a wider interest once an essential railway system was built.[37] Scrope was also a keen fisherman, and his record of fishing in the Tweed valley was reissued on several occasions late in the nineteenth century.[38] The grouse moors completed the trinity of hunting, shooting and fishing activities (Fig 15) which maintained land values and offered considerable employ-ment, albeit seasonal, to local smallholders. Exclusive sporting areas were built up, discouraging other visitors, but the ramblers were not to be denied. The Cuillins of Skye were explored in detail by Alexander Nicholson whose twenty years in the area, beginning in 1865, brought the first ascent of Sgurr Dubh Mor from Loch Coruisk in 1874. And although he failed in an attempt to secure the passage of an Access to the Mountains Bill in 1884, James Bryce did win a Commons resolution that legislation was needed to secure free access to uncultivated mountains and moorlands. Weekends and longer holidays in the country became more popular after World War I, encouraged by such inexpensive accommodation as that provided by the Scottish Youth Hostels Association. Motoring was growing in popularity, and by 1938 guidebooks were giving extensive cover to car tours, although lack of surfacing on many Highland roads limited the scope beyond Inverness. Since World War II, demand has greatly increased, calling for a massive expansion in accommod-ation and other facilities.

Substantial scenic endowment might be anticipated in the Outer Regions, with large tracts of sparsely settled hill country. But contrasts in rock type, complicated structural history and the heavy hand of glaciation have created remark-able diversity. Even the comparative monotony of landforms developed on the Moine and Dalradian metamorphic rocks, with accordant summit levels, is set off by the characteristically elongated salt- and fresh-water lochs, a further product of glaciation. The Highlands offer unrivalled grandeur with a remarkable amplitude of relief, but elsewhere there are attractive sequences of landscapes, with cultivated land grading into forest, grouse moor and mountain summit where rich alpine flora may attract interest, as on Ben Lawers near Fortingall (Perth & Kinross) where the National Trust for

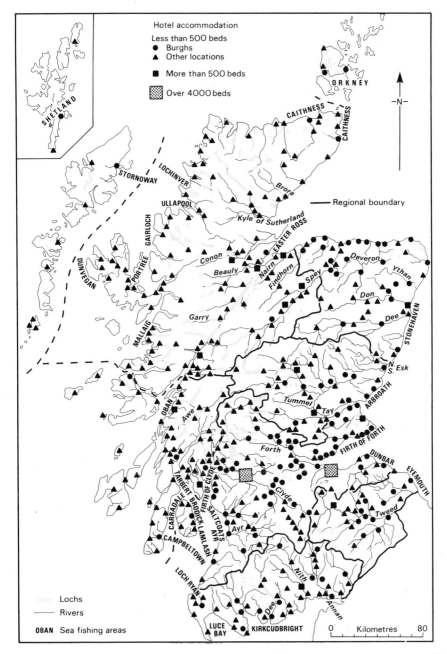

Fig 15 Salmon fishing and sea angling (Scottish Tourist Board)

Scotland have opened an information centre. Coastal scenery is similarly diverse, with such cliffs as Duncansby (Caithness) or the calm estuaries of Dumfries & Galloway. Scottish wildlife has a general touristical significance, reflected in the popularity of wildlife parks, and the 'Great Outdoors' has been coined as a suitable phrase to emphasise the scope for a range of sporting and recreational activities including sailing from Kippford and Kirkholm in Dumfries & Galloway, sand-yachting in Caithness, golfing on Dornoch Links (Sutherland), painting at Kirkcudbright, pony-trekking through the Borders or skiing on Cairngorm. The cultural landscape is a further key element in the touristical appeal of the Outer Regions.

The archaeological sites of Orkney and Shetland have a particular quality and fascination, although Iron Age and Pictish monuments on the mainland are significant and have probably not been sufficiently promoted.[39] However, the medieval legacy is far more compelling, and this has often been a major theme in tourist literature in the Borders.[40] But the Grampian endowment is equally fine with the castles of Craigievar and Kildrummy, abbeys of Deer and Kinloss, cathedrals of Elgin and Old Aberdeen (the latter restored for use as a parish church) and mansions such as Fyvie and Gordonstoun. Conservation areas have now been created in many towns, notably the Tayside group of Brechin, Forfar, Kerriemuir and Montrose, while villages, especially coastal fishing settlements, have received some planning protection — notably the 'string of pearls' from Auchmithie and St Vigeans in Angus to Boddam, Cairnbulg/Inverallochy and Port Erroll in Banff & Buchan, and Cullen, Findochty, Portessie, Portknockie and Portsoy in Moray. Moreover, local industry is not without its appeal; not only the forest walks and trails (Fig 16) but the Speyside whisky distilleries of Glenfarclas and Glenfiddich, the dairies in Kirkwall (Orkney) and Port Charlotte (Argyll & Bute) and a host of textile or craft industries are all of interest to the visitor.

The present regional picture of the tourist industry can be built up readily from information in handbooks (Table 8), but it is more difficult to present an adequate statistical summary of recent changes in the industry because few statistics have been produced consistently over a period of time. Until 1966 the Scottish Tourist Board gave estimates of the number of visitors to each county in Scotland, and while there are many inadequacies in this data it allows regions to be compared and trends to be discerned. It is evident that apart from a low figure for Angus and marginal positions for Banff, Berwick,

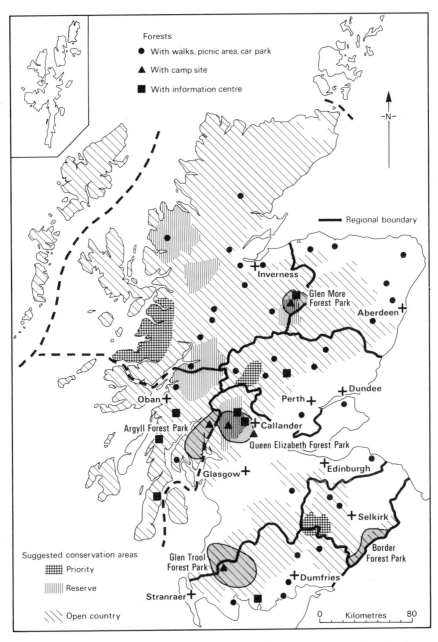

Forests

● With walks, picnic area, car park

▲ With camp site

■ With information centre

Regional boundary

Inverness

Glen More Forest Park

Aberdeen

Oban

Argyll Forest Park

Perth

Dundee

Callander

Queen Elizabeth Forest Park

Glasgow

Edinburgh

Selkirk

Border Forest Park

Glen Trool Forest Park

Dumfries

Stranraer

−N−

Suggested conservation areas

▦ Priority

▥ Reserve

▧ Open country

0   Kilometres   80

Fig 16. Forestry and recreation (<u>Forestry Commission</u>)

Table 8

THE TOURIST INDUSTRY: ADVERTISED ACCOMMODATION

Region	Number of Centres	Accommodation		a	b
		Total (000s)	Per centre (000s)		
Highland	259	23.03	0.09	8.5	23.2
Grampian	60	5.86	0.10	30.7	28.9
Tayside	48	6.32	0.13	20.9	40.7
NORTH	367	35.21	0.10	5.5	19.6
Borders	34	2.05	0.06	38.3	36.4
Dumfries & Galloway	46	3.59	0.08	15.9	39.8
SOUTH	80	5.64	0.07	10.1	31.2
OUTER REGIONS	447	40.85	0.09	4.8	16.9
CENTRAL BELT	186	26.84	0.14	29.5	26.5
SCOTLAND	633	67.69	0.11	11.7	14.5

(a) Percentage of total accommodation in largest centre; (b) percentage of total
accommodation in the next five largest centres

The largest centres are as follows: Highland: Inverness, Oban, Aviemore, Fort
William, Grantown on Spey; Grampian: Aberdeen, Ballater, Elgin — Lossiemouth,
Stonehaven, Braemar, Forres; Tayside: Pitlochry, Perth, Crieff, Auchterarder
(including Gleneagles), Dundee, Arbroath — Carnoustie; NORTH: Inverness, Aberdeen,
Oban, Pitlochry, Aviemore, Fort William; Borders: Peebles, Hawick, Galashiels,
Melrose, St Boswells, Kelso; Dumfries & Galloway: Dumfries, Stranraer — Portpatrick,
Moffat, Castle Douglas, Newton Stewart, Kirkcudbright; SOUTH: Dumfries, Peebles,
Stranraer — Portpatrick, Moffat, Castle Douglas, Newton Stewart; OUTER REGIONS: same
as North; CENTRAL BELT: Edinburgh, Glasgow, Ayr — Prestwick, Renfrew — Abbotsinch,
St Andrews, Largs; SCOTLAND: Edinburgh, Glasgow, Inverness, Aberdeen, Oban,
Ayr — Prestwick.
Note: percentage figures cannot be compared vertically without taking into account
the number of centres.
Source: Scottish Tourist Board Where to Stay in Scotland (1973 edition)

Orkney, Roxburgh, Selkirk and Shetland, all counties of the Outer Regions accommodated a higher share of Scotland's visitors than their population rating would warrant (with shares more than six times the population share in Bute, Inverness and Sutherland). When shares for 1963-6 are compared with those for two earlier four-year periods, it is evident that the trend is towards the Highlands and, to a lesser extent, the South. Thus the combined totals for Perth, Inverness, Ross & Cromarty and Sutherland rose from 22.19 per cent in 1955-8 to 25.31 in 1963-6, while the three counties constituting Dumfries & Galloway advanced from 3.81 to 4.75 per cent. The total share for the Outer Regions as a whole rose only slightly from 58.32 to 59.04 per cent, although both figures are greatly in excess of the total population share of 26.69 (1961). The reconstituted Scottish Tourist Board is compiling statistical data on a different basis; it is now revealed that occupancy rates in the Outer Regions are relatively low and that these regions attract a lower percentage of business visitors than holiday-makers (excluding Perth and Angus counties).

Although somewhat atypical, the accurate bed-night statistics presented in the annual reports of the Scottish Youth Hostel Association (SYHA) give some insight into local trends. In handling data over a period, difficulties arise because of changes in capacity and grade at particular hostels and, more importantly, through a steady turnover in hostel buildings. Leaving aside the popularity of Edinburgh, it is clear that the greatest increase in trade has been in the Aviemore area where the Association has recently made large investments in response to growing demand. By contrast, the southern fringes of the Highlands are becoming relatively less important as hostel members now have the means to travel further afield. But while most parts of the Highlands are increasing their shares of the total bed-nights, it is evident that the main centres attract growing custom. For Scotland as a whole the combined share of the ten largest hostels rose from 37.32 per cent in 1960-1 (two year average) to 42.35 in 1972-3. Conversely, closures tend to affect the intermediate category of hostel where substantial buildings are not attracting adequate custom; hence the 'failure' of Cruachan, between Crianlarich and Oban, and Elgin, between Aberdeen and Inverness. Fortunately for the remoter areas, the small hostel with simple buildings and low operating costs may well survive, given a willingness by a large organisation to cope with small units; and many simple hostels are now being provided outside the official SYHA organisation by education authorities and private organisations.[41]

Most tourist centres have developed piecemeal by a process
of accretion that is often not fully recorded. But a more
integrated approach can be seen in the expansion of deer
stalking, carving up the 'forests' into stalking beats with
accommodation provided in well-appointed lodges. Another early
form of planning for tourism concerns the railway hotel, the
most impressive example being Gleneagles, between Auchterarder
and Blackford (Perth & Kinross). The hotel opened by the London
Midland and Scottish Railway in 1924 completed the work begun
before World War I by the Caledonian Railway with the laying
out of golf courses. A still larger scale of operation is
brought out by the Cairngorm development where the Aviemore –
Coylumbridge – Glen More axis has been built up as the new
focus for tourism in the Highlands. The winter-sports facilities,
the principal recreational development, were built up gradually
over a period of two decades, the potential first being
appreciated during World War II when Norwegian Commandoes were
training in the area. In 1954 Karl Fuchs founded the Austrian
Ski School at Carr Bridge, and the following year the Scottish
Council for Physical Recreation (now the Scottish Sports
Council) expressed interest. Then the Cairngorm Winter Sports
Development Board was formed in 1957 to develop a national
winter-sports area, but growth came slowly and financial aid
from the HIDB was a major factor in achieving the development
of ski facilities, in 1966, needed to meet the rapid increase
in demand.

In the same year a new company was formed (Cairngorm Sports
Development Ltd), and the Board took debentures in it. Further
grant and loan assistance has been made since, and in 1971 the
Board purchased the upper slopes of Cairngorm from the
Forestry Commission. Meanwhile, accommodation was improved by
the Coylumbridge Hotel, opened in 1965, but most important is
the Aviemore Centre, a scheme envisaged by the late Lord Fraser
of Allander through the consortium of Highland Tourist
(Cairngorm Development) Ltd, formed in 1964. Opened in 1966 and
extended in 1972, the 12 hectare site contains various classes
of accommodation, together with catering services and shopping,
entertainment and sports facilities.

The contribution of the local authority was important in
developing the road to Glen More in 1961 and Coire Cas in 1966
(the road to Coire na Ciste, where ski facilities were opened
in 1973, was built by the Army in 1968), while the Forestry
Commission have assisted through the Forest Park, and the
Nature Conservancy are involved in the Achlean, Craigellachie
and Loch an Eilean nature trails. But the crucial factor was

the selective encouragement of support facilities by the HIDB
(hotels, wildlife park, visitor centre etc) which provided a
coherence previously lacking. By 1968 it was claimed that
Cairngorm was established as a 'highly developed ski area' with
first-class road access and facilities matched in few other
resorts.[42] The Winter Sports Festival, first organised in
1970-1, has helped promotion, and the successful British Ski
Championships in 1971-2 added to Aviemore's international status.
Even so, balancing accommodation and ski capacity has not been
satisfactorily achieved, and the conservation problems, arising
from litter and erosion on the mountain, have only slowly been
appreciated.[43] Commenting on the scheme, B. K. Parnell argues
that each facility is dependent on the simultaneous provision
of the rest: 'Aviemore has taken twenty years to develop, but
even if the needs and opportunity could not have been foreseen,
there was no organisation with the funds and powers to have
been able to plan a quicker and more satisfactory comprehensive
development.'[44]

     The Aviemore experience should be useful in promoting
smoother development in future. The 'model' of comprehensive
development was applied in a planning study of the Gairloch-
Poolewe area of Ross & Cromarty, but there has been no
implementation. However, the most recent attention has focused
on Aonach Mor near Fort William.[45] The mountain is close to
Ben Nevis and preferable to the latter for winter sports because
of better ski runs (high confidence levels for snow extend for
a slightly longer period than on Cairngorm) and an emotional
desire to avoid exploitation of the country's highest mountain.
Aonach Mor has also considerable potential for recreation in
summer, diverting some of the pressure from Ben Nevis and
Glencoe. Access to the slopes by cableway is proposed from a
base established along a narrow-gauge electric railway, which
could be provided by converting the British Aluminium Company's
industrial line which closed in 1971. Convenient for day visits
from the Central Belt, Fort William could be the first winter
resort to combine this traffic with the residential holiday
business, for a full range of accommodation and tourist
facilities is already available. The standard is generally
lower than at Aviemore, but this is because the summer season
is short, with tremendous pressure for some two months only.
A winter season could stimulate further investment and provide
more permanent employment.

     But looking beyond the individual project, a new dimension
on tourism planning is beginning to emerge through regional
and national coordination. The regional dimension is best

exemplified by the HIDB who immediately acted on guidelines
in the Scottish Plan that tourism should 'assist in consolidation
in some of the main centres and give a supplementary income to
the dispersed rural population engaged in primary and service
industry'.[46] The Board considered that 'the season must be
lengthened, visitor facilities of all kinds must be developed
to a high standard and through the Area Tourist Organisation an
efficient and friendly information service for the visitor must
be maintained'.[47] It is evident that the Board has given the
greatest attention to tourism, for by 1973 total grant and loan
assistance in this field was greater than for any other activity.
There has been a general concern to develop potential wherever
this may be located, but efforts have been made to promote
tourism at off-peak periods, to secure higher occupancy rates
in April – May and September – October, and to spread investment over a reasonably wide area. Special grant facilities have
now been withdrawn in the Badenoch and Inverness areas and are
restricted to a relatively low level in Fort William, Oban and
Ullapool, while in order to break the vicious circle created by
a gloomy perception of the potential for tourism tending to
limit growth through inadequate facilities, a special programme
of hotel building was initiated in the Islands. At the national
level the Scottish Tourist Board is active in the promotion
of tourism, but although a number of area-development studies
have been initiated, their implementation has been limited and
a basic national plan has not been provided.[48] There are still
no National Parks in Scotland, apart from Forest Parks,
National Nature Reserves and Country Parks, the latter largely
confined to the Central Belt, but five areas selected for their
'outstanding scenic beauty' were made subject to special
planning controls and the Countryside Commission for Scotland
now advises on selected applications for development.[49]
Discussion continues with National Parks as one element in an
overall strategy.

　　　Tourism plays a leading economic role in parts of the
Outer Regions, and in the Highlands it is claimed that 10 per
cent of the total labour force is employed in this way.[50] Yet
tourism is hardly an unmitigated blessing. Although the
tendency to disparage employment in tourism as 'menial' may be
deplored, because the occupation calls for personal qualities
and professional skills of a high standard, over-specialisation
in a highly seasonal activity brings its problems. Off-peak
custom at concessionary rates may enable some hotels in the
main centres (Fort William, Gatehouse of Fleet, Peebles,
Pitlochry and Ullapool, for example) to remain open through
the year, but the situation in rural areas may swing sharply

from a hectic summer period, with narrow roads congested with caravans, to a long winter when the permanent population, reduced in number by the demand for holiday cottages which now stand empty, may be hard pressed to maintain a sense of community. Environmental pressures develop and threaten to devalue the resources on which the industry depends, and while conflicts between different categories of tourist may be exaggerated, the accommodation of walkers in deer forests, canoers on salmon rivers and campers on farmland calls for skill and flexibility in land management and must imply acceptable limits which are properly integrated into a continuing planning exercise.[51] The enthusiasm by some individuals to drive tourism into the remotest corners of the Outer Regions, including such islands as Staffa and Tanera, should be tempered with caution and a careful regard for local operating conditions.

5

North Sea Oil and the Impact on Regional Development

This final chapter concentrates on the total industrial
geography of the Outer Regions and examines regional plans for
the accommodation of future growth. This includes consideration
of planning strategies for Scotland in which the problems and
potentials of the various Outer Regions are balanced against
the wider Scottish and British interests. At present the
uncertainties in the whole economic situation are compounded
locally by implications of offshore oil working which are
still far from clear. Since the oil industry has such a crucial
bearing on current regional trends, a summary of the situation
here is the first priority.

Fuel and Power Resources

A concise summary of the historical geography of fuel
supply by A. C. O'Dell emphasises the importance of coal move-
ments by land and sea.[1] East coast and Moray Firth ports
received a good deal of coal by sea in the eighteenth century,
and modest quantities were despatched round the Mull of Kintyre
to the West Highlands and round the Rhinns of Galloway to the
Solway creeks. The nineteenth century saw the distribution
system expanded to the Hebrides and the North Isles, while
inland districts, such as the Borders, were supplied by rail.
Over the years the relative importance of rail distribution has
increased, since apart from the special cases of islands or
mainland centres with very large demands, such as Aberdeen, rail
is a more flexible medium for supplying the various grades of
coal and smokeless fuels. This situation underlines the poverty
of the Outer Regions in valuable indigenous fuels. The most
important resources were found in the heavily faulted Sanquhar
Basin (Nithsdale) where output of good-quality coal was
stimulated by the railway to Dumfries, opened in 1850, only a
few years after the first Gatesdie pit was sunk. Fauldhead
colliery at Kirkconnel was opened in 1896. Production in 1950

amounted to 0.43 million ton (including the small surface working of Rig 1950-66), but Gateside closed in 1964 and Fauldhead in 1968, leaving only the Roger surface working, opened in 1953. At its heyday, the Sanquhar coalfield supported a considerable range of local industries.[2] This was also the case at the smaller outlying fields of coal, at Brora (Sutherland), Canonbie (Annandale & Eskdale) and Machrihanish (Argyll), where mining was carried on in the nineteenth century, continuing at Machrihanish until 1967 and Canonbie until 1922, and at Brora (where it was linked with brick making from Jurassic clays) until 1973. Other deposits were mentioned in gazetteers, but these never leant themselves to sustained mining.

Until comprehensive steamer and rail services were available, much of the North was forced to depend on wood and, more especially, peat. The thick mantles of peat found on the high ground in the Highlands, notably Caithness, and in the Dumfries & Galloway peat-flow regions, offer resources far in excess of domestic needs. Poor drainage and exposed climatic conditions make agricultural improvements financially unattractive, although for some years Altnabraec was the scene of experiments in peat-firing for thermal generation of electricity in 1959 and the HIDB have been urged to continue research, perhaps through further pilot schemes. However, there are substantial peat deposits in less-elevated situations, and these have been substantially modified in the course of agricultural development and domestic cutting for fuel. The greatest pressure, it seems, has been exerted on the low-level mosses, such as the Lochar Moss near Dumfries, and smaller fragments, such as Westhills Moss and Nutberry Moss, lying nearby on the Solway Plain.[3] Glacial interference exacerbated the natural drainage difficulty on the alluvial plain and thereby accelerated peat formation. Under the circumstances of a lowland environment, domestic fuel demands and the stimulus to improve have been heavy and the margins have been transformed. Likewise in parts of the Highlands coastal peat mosses, as in Lochaber at Keppoch (Arisaig), Blar Mor (Fort William) and Kentra (Acharacle), have been extensively transformed by peat cuttings and land reclamation for new crofts. In the Islands peat resources were not always adequate, and voyages were necessary to neighbouring communities. The people of Muck in the Small Isles cut peats in Ardnamurchan, in Shetland the islanders of Out Skerries had a right to peats on Whalsay (to supplement drift wood supplies) and in Orkney the islanders of Sanday would travel to the Calf of Eday for peats. Domestic fuel needs are now slight, although peat digging continues in crofting areas where labour is available. However, the distilleries still use peat to flavour the malt and this calls for a large scale of cutting, which can be observed in Islay and certain peaty interfluves in Moray.

Generation of hydroelectricity has been the greatest achievement in the energy field so far. Small generators (capacity below 1mw) for local supply were installed at several places at the turn of the century: Fochabers (Moray) and Inshes (Inverness) for example, but larger stations were built for extended supply areas following the example of the British Aluminium Company. The principal achievements in the North before World War II were the Grampian Scheme at Tummel/Rannoch, in Perth & Kinross (1928-33: - 42 mw) and the Scottish Power Company's project at Loch Luichart (Ross & Cromarty) 1926-34: - 36mw. Transmission lines linked the local distribution systems in the Grampian and Tayside regions, based on small thermal stations in the burghs, and led to the closure of the less-efficient producers (Fig 17). Further schemes in the Inverness and Lochaber districts, geared to local supply and electro-chemical industry, were defeated on amenity grounds.[4] The Caledonian Power Bill sought to harness the waters of Glen Garry and Glen Moriston to supply power to a calcium-carbide factory at Corpach (Fort William). But, whereas advocates of hydroelectricity in the 1930s envisaged development primarily for heavy power users (with potential ranging from 110mw in the 1918 survey to 556mw some twenty years later), the NSHEB (formed in 1943) has been concerned with comprehensive distribution.[5] The most important catchments over a period of some twenty years from 1945 were small schemes implemented to serve isolated localities in advance of grid connection (including diesel generators where no satisfactory hydro resources were available), but the main emphasis has been on fairly large stations generally, ranging in capacity from 20-60mw, to be fed into a much-extended national-grid system to help meet demand in the urban-industrial areas.[6] Such orthodox hydro schemes are no longer economically attractive, and all the best sites have by now been developed, but there remains a future for pumped storage schemes whose high capacities and low-load factors are ideal for meeting peak demand. Cruachan and Foyers (the latter a development of the original aluminium company installations) contribute 700mw capacity, but other forms of generation are needed.

The United Kingdom Atomic Energy Authority's (UKAE) proto-type fast reactor at Dounreay (Caithness) of 250mw now supplies the grid, and a further nuclear-power station, Stake Ness, (1,320mw), has been contemplated by the NSHEB. Thermal capacity is represented in Tayside by the Dundee plant, progressively extended to the present capacity of 307mw (including the 240mw

126

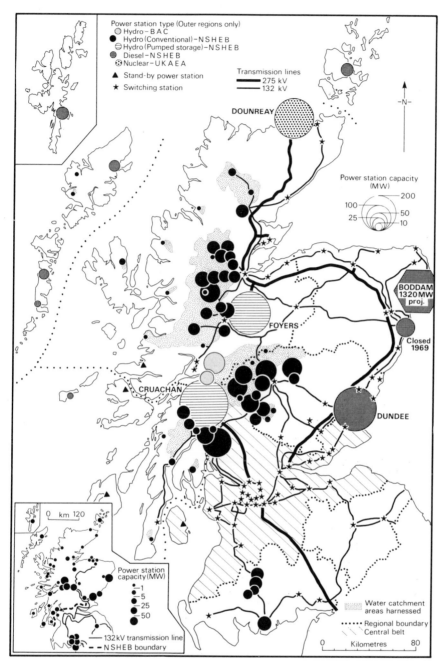

Fig 17. Electricity generation and distribution 1975
and (inset) 1948 (<u>NSHEB and SSEB</u>)

oil-fired Carolina Port 'B' station), and the Grampian region
(where Aberdeen's 57mw coal-fired plant was closed in 1969) by
the new oil-fired plant of 1320mw at Boddam, near Peterhead.
When this is completed, hydro capacity will represent only 59.1
per cent of a total capacity of 3,440mw, compared with 91.5
per cent in 1960 (955mw) and 78.3 in 1970 (1,830mw). Indigenous
resources are becoming less important, but power is widely
available in the Outer Regions and seldom acts as a constraint
on industrialisation, but some areas are still not connected
and a very heavy consumer (such as the British Aluminium
Corporation (BAC) at Invergordon) would not wish to stray far
from the 275kv transmission line. All the small local stations
in the South have been closed, and the only contributions to
the grid come from the UKAEA station at Chapelcross (Annandale
& Eskdale) with c. 300mw and the five hydro stations of the
Galloway scheme (1930-36), combined capacity 107mw, built to
operate with a low load-factor for peak support to the grid.

Oil from the North Sea is hardly likely to affect the
availability of power in the Outer Regions, but it will generate
considerable additional employment, and often in locations
outside the existing growth areas. The North Sea resources are
close to Western Europe, one of the most densely populated
industrial regions in the world. Moreover, the oil is owned and
controlled by these same countries, a political factor of no
mean significance. Our oil imports grew quickly after World War
II because of Europe's inability to produce sufficient coal
from indigenous sources as well as the demand for road transport,
which only oil could satisfy From this situation, there arose
in the late 1950s a large surplus of low-priced oil in the
Middle East, leading to a decline in coal mining and a further
increase in our dependence on that unstable area, a dependence
which hydroelectric power and nuclear energy, with all its
technical setbacks, have done little to reduce. Natural gas has
been of somehelp but not enough to prevent a strong lobby
calling for protection of the coal industry. The strong
nationalist forces in the Middle East have slowly reduced
Europe to the role of a consuming area for a vital commodity
produced in a region over which it exercised no real control.
Oil revenues to producer countries are now greatly in excess of
total production costs and oil-company profits, although not,
as yet, oil-taxation revenue in consuming countries.
Unexpectedly high demand for oil in 1970, not to mention
aggravation of transport problems, gave the producing countries
a much stronger bargaining position which they are using to
increase their income and to demand a stake in the equity of
the major companies.

The general sequence of events in the industry need only be summarised here. The discovery of natural gas at Slochteran in the Netherlands suggested that further supplies might be trapped under the Permian sandstone in a geological structure extending across the North Sea. Improved survey methods were employed in the southern sector, and licences allocated in the British sector (whose limits were settled by international convention, effective in 1964) led to a series of discoveries between 1965 and 1972. Structures in the northern sector offered the possibility of oil, and the distribution of the licensed areas indicated a growing interest in the area after 1964. The risk of very severe weather and the greater depths of water have called for more durable and sophisticated equipment which has only made all-year drilling possible in Shetland waters in the last few years.

Initial discoveries in the Norwegian sector, Cod and Ekofisk in 1968 and 1969 respectively, were followed by successes in the British sector in 1969, Montrose field, and in 1970, Josephine and Forties fields. Then the Argyll, Auq and Montrose fields were discovered in 1971, along with the first major find in Shetland waters, the Brent field. The 1972 finds of Beryl, Cormorant and Thistle were again in this most northerly area and the same pattern continued in 1973 (Alwyn, Dunlin, and Hutton), and in 1974 (Magnus and Ninian), with Claymore Piper and Maureen further south (Fig 18). Drilling continues, but already there is a prospect of a total output from all the known fields of 175 million ton per annum, and this supports the claim that Britain may be a net oil exporter in the early 1980s. However, some fields have proved disappointing in that large structures, such as Cormorant, are complex and do not necessarily contain a very big pool of oil. There have also been delays in developing the fields. In view of its overriding national importance, production will be forced ahead as quickly as possible, certainly until the early 1980s. Exploration, however, will probably settle down to a more mature rate now that most of the major structures are accounted for. 'But drilling in the new areas of the West Shetlands and the Celtic Sea are only just starting up, and the whole range of future possibilities is widening all the time, while high prices and energy demand have greatly increased the range of finds that can be considered economic.'[7] In addition to the oil, however, with successes extending over the sector boundary into Norwegian waters, there are the gasfields (both associated, with oil, and non-associated): Frigg stands astride the boundary (and will be delivering 1,500 million cu ft per day by the late 1970s), while Heimdall, exclusively in Norwegian waters, is balanced by the 'Total' discovery on the

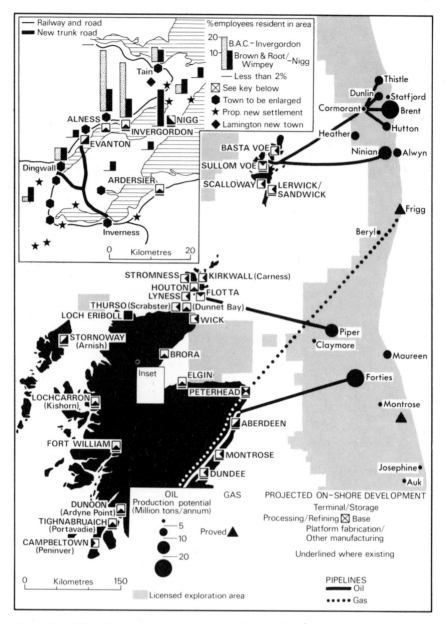

Fig.18. Oil discoveries and developments (<u>Various sources including HIDB, NESDA and Dr G.A. Mackay, Aberdeen University</u>)

British side — and gas may well be found in the western basins where exploration is only just beginning.

   The new oil wealth raises important political questions, such as the extent to which the proceeds should be earmarked for investment in the producing regions, and fiscal policy has to balance the government case for a fair share of the profits against the risk of discouraging exploration and inhibiting production from marginal fields. But here the main concern is with the onshore geography arising from the activity at sea. First to be considered is the constant demand during exploration and production for service bases which will be sought at ports combining proximity to the offshore area with adequate capacity. Aberdeen has been most successful, with several hundred firms established in the city and substantial harbour development plans being carried out, but Dundee and Peterhead are also very active. Activity further north has brought Lerwick and Sandwick (Shetland) into play, while the westward drift in exploration activity has focused interest on Stornoway, with further prospects for Caithness, Orkney and Sutherland. Second, the development of the oilfields over the next ten to fifteen years will depend very heavily on the firms fabricating production platforms which, unlike the 'semi-submersible' drilling rigs, must be rooted to the sea-bed. As the preference appears to be for locations near the potential fields with good communications and sheltered inshore waters, the Highlands come very strongly into the picture because not only have they the advantage of proximity to the oilfields, minimising the towing operations, but there are coastal sites which provide either the extensive areas of flat land (80 hectares at Nigg in Ross and Cromarty) needed for horizontal fabrication of steel platforms, or the deep sheltered water (up to 30 fathoms close inshore for first stage assembly and as much as 120 fathoms further out) for the vertical building of concrete structures as proposed for Loch Carron in Wester Ross. Steel platforms are expensive. The 'Highland One' platform, completed at Nigg Bay in 1974, used 50,000 ton of steel and cost £50 million. By contrast, the concrete platform costs only £20 million and by incorporating oil storage could, in some marginal cases, eliminate the need for a pipeline. But despite the simplicity and versatility of the concrete designs, especially 'Condeep', doubts over the ultimate performance and environmental problems will ensure a continuing demand for steel structures. Third, the production of the oil requires land-based facilities for storage and processing. Although arrangements will be made at the smaller fields to transfer oil direct to a tanker which may then take the oil to destinations outside Scotland, the larger fields can only be harnessed efficiently by pipeline to the coast. Forties oil will come ashore at Cruden Bay (Banff & Buchan), while Piper (and no doubt Claymore also) will be connected to Flotta (Orkney), and pipes to Sullom Voe (Shetland) will connect up with the Cormorant and Ninian groups. A further pipeline will take Frigg gas to St Fergus (Banff & Buchan), and this same pipe could connect up with other gas fields in the area.

Although the pipes to the mainland will continue straight on to processors or consumers elsewhere, there is a definite prospect of an ammonia factory at Peterhead based on natural gas.[8] The island terminals will certainly require storage facilities, pending transfers to tankers, and the development of refining is a possibility. Scotland's only oil refinery is at Grangemouth in the Central Belt but proposals for further capacity, based originally on Scotland's wealth of potential industrial sites served by deep-water anchorages (notably the Cromarty Firth and Firth of Clyde), are now being further stimulated by the prospect of very substantial oil production and a government desire that up to two-thirds of the oil found should be refined in the UK. Campbeltown and Sullom Voe have attracted interest, and the Cromarty Petroleum application for Nigg (Ross & Cromarty) follows no less than three previous soundings during the postwar period.[9] Also very significant is the underwater testing base at Fort William, the training centre at Montrose and the proposed offshore maintenance centre for Caithness.

Regional Planning in Scotland

Postwar problems of industrial diversification were recognised as being particularly pressing in the Tayside area. But for the Outer Regions as a whole the greatest need was for a larger industrial sector to reduce the depopulation arising from the contraction of primary industries. A greater pace of industrial development is required, and this effort has been gradually extended since the first initiatives when the North of Scotland Hydroelectric Board was set up and a Highland Development Area created round the Inner Moray Firth. But in the early 1960s, despite the completion of electrification in all but the remoter areas and the extension of Development Area status to most parts of the Outer Regions, the problems of net out-migration were still causing concern.[10] A review of the 1950 White Paper observed that 'the establishment of light manufacturing industries has ... proved a most difficult task'.[11] A fresh impetus was needed, and government activity has intensified over the last ten years. The publication of the Scottish Plan in 1966 marked the first attempt to develop a growth strategy for both the Central Belt and the Outer Regions; although the Central Belt was to receive most attention in the short term, there was a clear view of expansion in growth areas of the North during the 1970s and the regrouping of settlement in the rural areas with concentration of investment 'on the points identified as centres of the main labour catchment areas and on those villages and townships in the hinterland which offer the best hope of viability'.[12] The Scottish Plan picked out the principal Highland labour catchments: the Inverness, Fort William and Wick-Thurso areas as well as Campbeltown, Dunoon, Golspie-Brora, Kirkwall, Lerwick, Lochgilphead, Oban and Stornoway.[13] In the North-east potential development centres were identified in Aberdeen, Banff-Macduff, Buckie, Elgin, Fraserburgh, Huntly, Keith and Peterhead.[14]

In 1969 the Gaskin Report argued that to avoid excessive fragmentation of effort, growth might be related to four groupings, to focus on Aberdeen, Banff-Macduff, Elgin and Peterhead-Fraserburgh. However, 'given the difficulties facing the region, and in view of the limited amount of mobile industry and the intense inter-regional competition for it, there is a clear need to concentrate planning efforts to achieve the maximum impact on the attractiveness of the region for potential incoming industry'. Therefore, it was thought inadvisable to promote four zones simultaneously, and for the immediate future Aberdeen was to claim the 'preponderence of regional planning effort' with Elgin as the focus of a second-ary growth area extending outwards to Buckie and Forres.[15] This latter area could be associated with the Inner Moray Firth area, selected by the HIDB as the most promising growth area in their territory; but Lochaber and Caithness also seemed capable of attracting large-scale industry. Lochaber already has two major industries, an aluminium smelter and a pulp-paper mill, but some 'second-generation' problems, concerning jobs for school leavers and women, need attention and further factory sites are being developed.[16] The capacity in Caithness arises from the growth of services in connection with the Dounreay experimental reactor station and the further expansion through the present construction of the prototype fast reactor. In view of the likelihood of a run-down in employment there, in the 1970s, coordinated action has been taken since 1968 to provide industrial opportunities, and growth is proceeding at both Thurso and Wick. The special advantages of the Aberdeen and Inner Moray Firth areas were underlined by the Scottish Plan in 1966 when a holding and consolidation operation was envisaged with a view to more sustained development in the future when more pressing problems in the Central Belt had been

dealt with and communications with the North improved.[17] The
other Outer Regions, recognised under the system of planning
subregions of 1964, were thoroughly studied, although the degree
of elaboration varied considerably. In the Borders the
expansion of St Boswells was expected, while in Dumfries &
Galloway most of the marginal population increase was expected to
accrue to Dumfries and other towns in the eastern sector of the
region.[18] The Tayside study was one of a group of three
estuarine studies.[19] The proposal to concentrate most of the
future growth on Dundee and Perth contrasts with the thrust of
the earlier study of G. Payne which anticipated that the wartime
decentralisation of industry would continue and provide
opportunities for the smaller settlements.[20]

    But thinking was also veering towards the idea of special
development authorities, especially for the Highlands. In 1955
F. F. Darling stated that 'effective rehabilitation will call
for an organisation with executive authority able to act in
several fields'.[21] In 1964 the Highland Panel drew attention
to the fact that more than thirty government departments and
agencies were concerned with the Highlands for economic and
social purposes; they suggested 'considerable rationalising and
streamlining of the administrative machinery, including the
allocation of money for Highland affairs'.[22] In recognition of
an election pledge made by the Labour Party calling for special
promotional measures, the HIDB was set up in 1964, replacing
the purely advisory panel of experts which had assisted the
Secretary of State in matters relating to the Highlands and
Islands since 1947. The new authority was to operate a scheme
of grants and loans for the promotion and development of industrial and commercial concerns. This was the first time that a
regional agency of government in the UK had been given such
power. Previously no one body possessed the financial resources
and powers to undertake, in a comprehensive manner, the essential
task of attracting new industries to the Highlands and Islands.[23]
The Board have recently defined their objectives in this field;
definition of resources and publicity to attract developers,
assistance to industrialists by way of advice, better facilities
and even advance factories, encouragement to expand existing
industries and developments of crafts where larger-scale
industry would be unlikely.[24] In view of the Board's considerable powers, it is rather surprising to find that their area of
responsibility is arbitrarily determined, following the seven
'Crofting Counties' which were accorded special treatment in
1886 because the main crofting areas lay within them. Other
rural areas, such as the islands of Arran and Bute and the
uplands of the Grampian and Tayside regions, might well have

qualified for similar assistance, but the only modifications have been the inclusion of Arran and Bute and areas outside the Crofting Counties assigned to the Highland Region in 1975.

But elsewhere there were no special incentives. This was to some extent understandable because of some success in industrial development. Also, as a prominent local economist argued for the Grampian region, that area was compact with a fairly healthy population structure and a major city as its regional capital. This was not the picture of an area incapable of producing its own incentives. Furthermore, special financial and other inducements 'are a slippery slope that can only lead regional policy into an irrational morass of special (and competing) cases'.[25] A unified approach has emerged from within the region through the North-east Development Committee (including Aberdeen City, Aberdeen County and Kincardine County). This organisation was enlarged to cover the whole region as a result of a recommendation in 1969 for a more comprehensive body and encouragement from the Scottish Office. The task of this North-east Scotland Development Authority is 'to assist and encourage companies to settle in the area; to encourage existing industry to expand and take advantage of new opportunities; to ensure that the rural economy and the traditional industries are kept in perspective with new developments; and to act as a link between local authorities in these matters'.[26] Like the regional coordination of planning, handled by a separate organisation, this function has been taken over by the Grampian regional council, but the successful NESDA organisation has been retained to serve the new administration. There was some speculation that the HIDB might have been run down or disbanded with the completion of the local government reform, but this was not well founded.

The Scottish Plan of 1966 has never been revised or updated. However, the broad strategy of growth areas continues to win tacit approval. The Scottish Council (Development and Industry) argue that 'modest growth at Galashiels should continue to consolidate the population of the Borders; and in Dumfries & Galloway the growth of light manufacturing round Dumfries should have the same effect (and 'in the longer term there is good opportunity for the establishment of a major new urban area based on the UK potential of the Solway Firth').[27] In the Highlands, the growth prospects of the Moray Firth area are underlined; while Aberdeen and Dundee have sufficient potential to warrant a national strategy, adopting the concept of a new axis from Ayr to Aberdeen, supplementing the existing urban axis of the Central Belt. 'Most of the population growth for which ... it is realistic to plan by the end of the century, together with related industrial developments, should be located in the line of this axis.'[28] A Select Committee thought that the Scottish Office should consider the view that some of the Outer Regions (especially the Grampian and Highland regions) might benefit from the designation of a 'modest-sized new town', to improve the image of the area and build up labour catchments attractive to industrialists.[29] Although the selection involved in a growth-area policy can be politically embarrassing, it is clear that local authorities appreciate the economies which follow from concentration of investment in areas which are coming under pressure from industries seeking out attractive sites close to deep water. The expansion in the average size of oil tanker and ore carrier has brought an interest to some of the remoter rural regions which the Scottish Plan could hardly have foreseen when optimism for the future of the Outer Regions was expressed in such guarded terms. Large-scale developments thus constitute a unique bonus to be invested carefully so as to develop a new regional structure.

But caution is required because not only are the growth areas much too small for the 'growth-pole' theory of the economists to be relevant, but linkages tend to be weak (associated activities do not tend to coalesce around a 'propulsive industry') and commuting areas are very limited. Although little research has been done on the latter point, evidence from census material and from studies of large firms in Ross & Cromarty indicates that expansion of population related to a large industrial development will tend to fall within a very limited area (Fig 18 inset, see p130). Fort William has a large catchment area for timber supplies to its two mills (Fig 19), but these units draw almost all their workers from the immediate vicinity and even such villages as North Ballachulish and Spean Bridge are poorly represented. Admittedly, in Fort William's case the settlement pattern in Lochaber is hardly conducive to a large number of workers travelling from places 15-25km away, and the physical potential at such intermediate distances much too limited for dispersal of planned population growth to be feasible. But round the Invergordon area Tain, Strathpeffer and Dingwall are limits beyond which commuting seems to take place only with a degree of reluctance. The implication is that the 'spread' effect around a growth pole is likely to be skin deep and that over wide areas the growth area will have a parasitic function, drawing the surplus labour away to new housing estates at the factory doorstep. People from Caithness and Lewis, for example, work in Invergordon, spending only their weekends at home, while movement of local people to new and better-paid employment

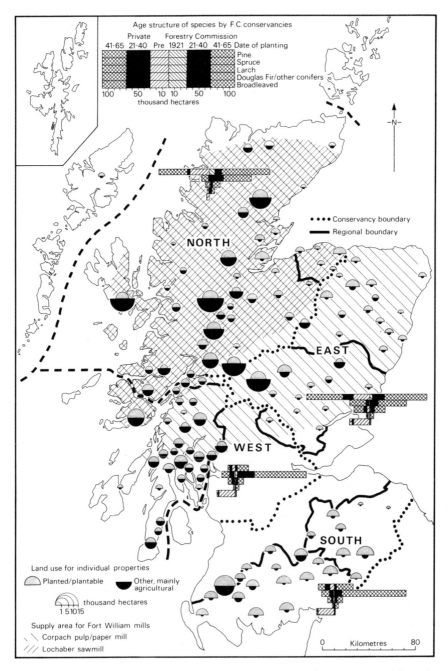

Age structure of species by F.C. conservancies

Private | Forestry Commission
41-65 21-40 | Pre 1921 21-40 41-65 | Date of planting

Pine
Spruce
Larch
Douglas Fir/other conifers
Broadleaved

100   50   10 10   50   100
thousand hectares

•••• Conservancy boundary
━━━ Regional boundary

NORTH

EAST

WEST

SOUTH

-N-

Land use for individual properties

⬗ Planted/plantable   ◖ Other, mainly
                              agricultural

thousand hectares
1 5 10 15

Supply area for Fort William mills
╲ ╲ Corpach pulp/paper mill
╱╱╱ Lochaber sawmill

0   Kilometres   80

Fig 19. Forestry Commission properties and timber supplies to Fort William (Forestry Commission, Scottish Pulp & Paper Mills and Messrs Riddoch of Rothiemay)

with the incoming industry may create vacancy chains which suck in not only the remaining unemployed but other workers from outside. Easter Ross farmers have lost labour to the aluminium smelter, and while this has provided them with an incentive to streamline their methods and increase mechanisation it has required some search for new labour and farm workers have come south from Caithness and Orkney. It might well be agreed that a holding of population in the Invergordon area was preferable to emigration from the north and west going out of the Highlands altogether, but in this case growth centres are merely redirecting (and possibly accelerating) migration flows.

The rural problem embraces two related questions. First, are there labour catchments orientated to small burghs that can attract 'spread effects' from growth areas? The largely autonomous economic recovery experienced in the Grampian region in the late 1960s, with growth in distilling, fishing, food processing and textiles and reduced labour shedding in agriculture, contributed to the growth of small towns there. Turriff, with a long-standing tradition in agricultural engineering, attracted firms dealing with carbon papers, knitwear and meat packing. The attraction of small central places might be strengthened by a form of grouping of interrelated burghs as in Moray and perhaps the Badenoch and Strathspey settlements of Carr Bridge, Aviemore, Kingussie and Newtonmore. The restructuring of rural settlement can then be related to new employment opportunities in the local centres and studies have been completed for parts of the Borders (Berwickshire) and Grampian (Buchan) regions, although in the latter case several attempts have been needed to find a compromise between the economic benefits of concentration and the social demand for a greater spread of development (Fig 20).[30]

There are very extensive rural areas, especially in the Highlands, which cannot be linked with a small town. Although there are a surprisingly large number of small industries located in these sparsely settled areas, they are mostly concerned with craft industries, food processing and maintenance, and employment is inadequate to arrest migration, especially in the context of attractive job opportunities and high wages elsewhere (Fig 21). Studies have been made of some possible rural-development areas in the Highlands, and the Speyside area of Moray has also been investigated, but the only progress in the foreseeable future lies in the coordination of local-authority investment in housing and services and selective development of primary industries.[31] The Western Isles may well be an exception because of a relatively large, active and

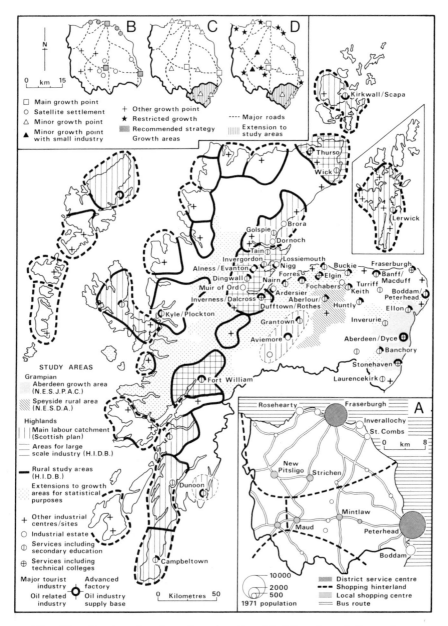

B **C** **D**

N
0 km 15

☐ Main growth point   + Other growth point   --- Major roads
○ Satellite settlement   ★ Restricted growth   ⫴ Extension to
△ Minor growth point   ▨ Recommended strategy   study areas
▲ Minor growth point   Growth areas
   with small industry

Kirkwall/Scapa

Lerwick

Thurso
Wick

Brora
Golspie
Dornoch
Tain
Invergordon   Lossiemouth   Buckie   Fraserburgh
Alness/Evanton   Forres   Elgin   Banff/
Dingwall   Nairn   Fochabers Turriff Macduff
Muir of Ord   Keith   Boddam/
Ardersier   Aberlour   Huntly   Peterhead
Inverness/Dalcross   Dufftown/Rothes   Ellon
Kyle/Plockton   Nigg
                    Grantown   Inverurie
                Aviemore   Aberdeen/Dyce
                                          Banchory
STUDY AREAS   Stonehaven
Grampian
  Aberdeen growth area   Laurencekirk
  (N.E.S.J.P.A.C.)
  Speyside rural area
  (N.E.S.D.A.)
Highlands
⫴ Main labour catchment
  (Scottish plan)
  Areas for large
  scale industry (H.I.D.B.)
━ Rural study areas
  (H.I.D.B.)
  Extensions to growth
  areas for statistical
  purposes
+ Other industrial   Fort William
  centres/sites
○ Industrial estate
⫾ Services including
  secondary education
⊕ Services including
  technical colleges

Major tourist   Advanced
industry   factory   Dunoon
Oil related   Oil industry
industry   supply base   0 Kilometres 50
                                  Campbeltown

A
Rosehearty   Fraserburgh
                        Inverallochy
                        St. Combs
New   0 km 8
Pitsligo   Strichen
                Mintlaw
        Maud   Peterhead
                        Boddam
  ◯ 10000   ▨ District service centre
  ○ 2000   --- Shopping hinterland
    500   ⫴ Local shopping centre
1971 population   ═ Bus route

Fig 20. Regional planning in the Highland and Grampian
regions (<u>HIDB and NESDA</u>)

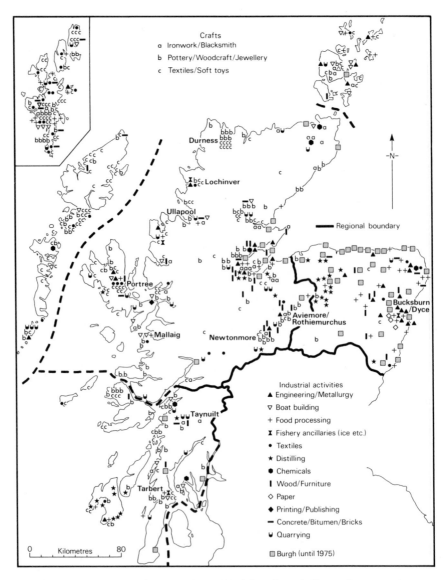

Fig 21. Rural industry in the Highland and Grampian regions
(HIDB and NESDA)

community-conscious population wishing to start small rural projects. The Highland Fund has made 'character loans' totalling £700,000 since 1954 at nominal rates of interest and the bulk of the assistance has gone to the Islands, with substantial aid to agriculture and fishing. Although the Fund consciously leans towards the Highlands rather than other areas of rural Scotland, the distribution of loans is basically a response to the demand for help with rural projects. In the Uists the growth of facilities on Benbecula will include secondary education and an improved range of shops, thereby strengthening the island community as a whole, but it is doubtful if the sense of gain at this community level will always be appreciated against the local sacrifices that are implicit in the selection process.[32]

The Impact of Oil-related Industry

The speed of development, maintained at a high level in the national interest, has brought new problems and opportunities to the North. 'Few regions of the UK, if any, can have experienced such a sudden and total reversal of lowly fortunes as has been witnessed in the north-eastern shoulder of Scotland during the past few years.'[33] The increase in employment in the Grampian region between 1971 and 1981 is expected to be about 34,000, and since most of the jobs will have to be filled by immigrants to the area the total population may increase by 50,000.[34] Although it remains to be seen whether or not the new Grampian regional authority will encourage the highest possible rate of growth, even a low estimate of population increase will mean an increase of 23,000 over 1971.[35] This compares with a decrease of 3,600 indicated in the projection of the Scottish Development Department (SDD), published as recently as 1972.[36] In the Highlands, where the SDD estimate provided for a small increase of 3,600, an increase of employment of 15,000 is now expected and this would be even more dependent on immigration. The total increase in population could exceed 30,000, (and this excludes Argyll & Bute). But despite the profound implications, the accommodation of all the new growth has been left very largely to local authorities, but in the Highlands the infrastructural weaknesses have brought a stronger government response, with aid for the improvement of the main road from Perth to Inverness and for its extension directly northwards across the firths. Conservational problems have been encountered in the Highlands because of the pressure on coastal sites for production platform building. A general discussion document has been followed by a more explicit policy document setting out the preferred conservation and development zones.[37]

Because the oil industry 'must be grafted on to the old industrial areas of Clyde and Forth, to regenerate their declining economies', it seemed clear that the Firth of Clyde would become the main area for platform building with sites at Hunterston (Strathclyde) and Portavadie and Macringan's Point (both in Argyll & Bute) joining the established yard at Ardyne Point (also in Argyll & Bute).[38] With further possibilities in the refining field, the net effect could be a significant reduction in pressure on areas further north, although the competition for labour will not be appreciated by some local firms, such as the Campbeltown Shipyard, whose growth prospects may be undermined by the erosion of their labour force. On the other hand any reduction of the high unemployment rate in Campbeltown would be desired, and this reinforces the positive contribution of oil-related industry to regional planning: it may offer the economic stimulus for the extension of the limited growth area pattern. However during 1975 it became clear that the demand for production platforms would be smaller than anticipated. Ardyne Point had spare capacity while Portavadie, the only other site on the Firth of Clyde actually developed, was still awaiting its first order at the end of 1975.

In the Grampian region the oil developments have created further confidence in Aberdeen and promotional work is now hailing the port, not only as the core of Scotland's Middle East, but as the offshore capital of Europe, likely to account for 35,000 of the expected population increase of 50,000 by 1981. As the largest urban concentration in the North, Aberdeen naturally has important advantages in terms of services and labour supply. The local fishing industry has generated marine services over the last century, and hence the basis of a specialised infrastructure is already present. In the context of the oil workings, Aberdeen is not always the nearest port but it is the nearest major port and has, therefore, attracted the bulk of the service and the demands of the oil companies have resulted in a large development project for Aberdeen Harbour, enabling services to be available at all states of the tide. A number of firms have built their marine headquarters close to the harbour (Amoco, Shell, Texaco and Total) and other companies have substantial administrative headquarters in the area including Amoco and Shell at Tullos Estate, BP at Farburn Estate, Dyce and Total at Altens. Major supply and warehousing firms include Aberdeen Service Company, Christian Salvesen, Hudson's Freight, John Wood and Seaforth Maritime, and four American companies have established oil-tool factories in the Aberdeen area to supply the Eastern Hemisphere: Baker Oil Tools,

Smith International, Vetco Offshore and Weatherford Oil Tools. South Eastern Drilling Services have a shore base and training school, while British Airways Helicopters and Bristow Helicopters are established at Dyce. But the estimated total oil-related investment in Aberdeen of some £50 million, however, includes a very large number of relatively small ventures.

The provision of new housing will be concentrated into the zone immediately adjacent to the present built-up area (10,000 houses) with 1,900 in Banchory and Stonehaven, 2,400 in Inverurie, and 300 in Ellon.[39] This compares with the earlier plan of 1969 with 3,300 houses in the Aberdeen suburban area (concentrated in Dyce) and 2,400 in Inverurie.[40] However, some growth is extended to other ports: BP and Conoco have their marine bases in Dundee, and both Aberdeen Service Company (including accommodation for the Phillips group) and Arunta have facilities at Peterhead. Although the great majority of the smaller services are based in Aberdeen, there is some spread: Banchory Instruments, W. H. Wilson at Ellon (pipeline components), R. B. Farquhar at Huntly (portable offices), Versatile Steel at Inverurie (storage hoppers), Speyside Engineering at Elgin (components) and Tamworth Industrial Fabrics at Forres. Thus the oil industry will certainly justify a broader location policy of growth in Elgin, Fraserburgh and Peterhead, in addition to Aberdeen, although it is doubtful if it would be realistic to envisage expansion in all small towns and stability in rural areas too. Continuing internal migration seems very likely.

In the Highlands the Moray Firth area has proved attractive for oil-related industry, and this growth area may take up to 60 per cent of the increase in employment and population. The area has developed thanks to the attention drawn to its resources by the HIDB, through their Moray Firth Development strategy, at a time when new aluminium smelters were being considered in Britain. The area was closely studied by the HIDB in 1966 and 1967, leading to the commissioning of the Jack Holmes Planning Group to produce a plan demonstrating the important considerations which would have to be faced in providing facilities and environment for the long-term growth of population based on industrial expansion.[41] Late in 1967 the county council submitted amendments to their development plan, allowing for industrial development at Invergordon and housing at Alness, where the scale of new growth has created a virtually new community. Oil-related activity, particularly platform building, has come into the Invergordon area and brought a substantial population increase. Although much of

143

the demand for housing is temporary and is, therefore, being met by caravans and the use of cruise ships, there will be sufficient permanent expansion for the creation of another new community at Lamington, between Invergordon and Tain, as well as the growth of the main existing settlements.[42] Invergordon and its associated dormitories will have a 'dumb-bell' relationship with Inverness which continues to develop its range of services, including technical training, which might ultimately develop into a Highland university. The fabrication yard at Ardersier is increasing demand for housing in Nairn.

The Olsen Stornoway base underpins the leading centre of the Outer Hebrides (although one currently losing population), the various base proposals in Orkney bolster the island capital of Kirkwall, and the Loch Carron platform sites may be related to Kyle-Kyleakin, a possible 'new-town' location but one previously lacking in economic potential. Oil-related developments may be used constructively to restructure the hierarchy of settlement and services, and hence the regional significance of new proposals should form an important part of the assessment. Despite the apparent lack of a strong lead from the centre, local efforts are exploiting the benefits. In Shetland, where the advent of oil 'endangered the carefully nurtured economy as well as the social fabric of the island and the physical environment',[43] the county council has confidentially sought effective control of development with industry to be steered to Sullom Voe, where 1,000 jobs is seen as a 'fairly realistic' estimate, and housing provided in the enlarged communities of Brae, Voe and Mossbank-Toft. Orkney, like Shetland, is promoting a private parliamentary bill to control development by designating appropriate areas and taking harbour powers in Scapa Flow. Growth will fall short of the level at which 'an overbalance of the present life of Orkney' might be experienced.

Housing development on Orkney's mainland, especially in Kirkwall and Stromness, is seen as preferable to expansion on the smaller islands. And in Wester Ross it is likely that the site limitations of Kyle would lead to a 'necklace' of development extending from Kyle to Balmacara, Dornie and Lochcarron, leaving aside temporary workers accommodated in hostels or cruise liners hired for the purpose. Virtually all the arguments bearing on the theme of Highland development were thoroughly aired in 1974 at the public enquiry into the proposal to establish a yard for concrete platforms at Drumbuie on the southern side of Loch Carron. Although the national interest in a domestic capacity in this field was a prominent element in the enquiry, it is possible to spotlight the purely local controversy, balancing the need for employment and the logic of growth in the Kyle area against the irreparable damage to the community on account of the large scale of the new industry envisaged.[44] The Drumbuie application failed, but despite the desire for a conservation zone along the west Highland coast, a subsequent application by Howard-Doris for a development at Kishorn has been approved and work on a concrete platform is progressing.[45] Already new housing has appeared at Lochcarron and the railway from Inverness to Kyle has gained welcome new traffic.

Conclusion

The Highland situation is clearly encouraging. Growth is coming from oil-related industries, but other chapters in this book have drawn attention to favourable trends in fishing, textile manufacture, tourism and other activities. Underpinned by the assistance of the HIDB, the last decade has brought an increase in population which, although modest in absolute terms, is significant in reversing the downward trend evident at every census from 1841 to 1961. The settlement pattern is receiving its biggest fillip in modern times and this may generate more coherent catchment areas for services and employment, providing that change can be harmonised with the aspirations of the existing communities and reasonable amenity safeguards. The Board's work is not universally acclaimed, mainly because the growth-area policy has meant little respite for those remoter areas which continue to lose population. Resources may be exploited with assistance from the Board, but they cannot be manipulated to create new jobs in strict proportion to local needs; and although it is appreciated that 'the Board will be judged by its ability to hold population in the true crofting areas', no firm policy on population has been laid down and overall trends in the region will continue to obscure sharp contrasts in different areas.[46]

Yet it is important that a local-development plan should be pursued further. Although compromised by the centralising forces of large-scale oil-related industries and by the failure of some small industries faced with the national recession, some coordinated programme of HIDB promotion, local authority investment and transport provision by the national-ised undertakings is needed. Even with perfect coordination the local centres thus identified and supported will be subject to many continuing uncertainties concerned with optimum levels of centralisation of housing and education and subsidy of industry and transport. But this is no justification for not attempting greater sophistication and sensitivity in planning.

The problem is greatest in the Highlands and Islands since the population is more scattered and the islands have their own situation.[47] Yet in the other Outer Regions, too, industrial development is most evident in the main growth centres, leaving rural areas to suffer depopulation which, exacerbated by repeated cuts in services, may be self-perpetuating.[48] New initiatives to deal with rural problems are being taken in various parts of Scotland, but whereas there is a general appreciation of the advantages and limitations of the growth-centre approach in planning, the rural counterpart is not nearly so well understood and much work remains tentative and exploratory. There is scope here for a contribution from the academic world and the establishment at Aberdeen University of an Institute for the Study of Sparsely Populated Areas is an encouraging development.[49] The Outer Regions are on their way to eliminating their poverty in manufacturing industries inherited from the nineteenth century. The regions affected by oil-related developments show the trend most dramatically, with traditional net migration flows showing a refreshing, although probably short-term, change in direction. But, perhaps inevitably, the price of this progress in diversification has been a neglect of the potential in rural areas. This problem should now be tackled on a broader front for it is prominent as the main outstanding element in the postwar modernisation of the Outer Regions. To this extent the claim that these peripheral areas constitute part of the 'New Scotland' remains to be vindicated.

Acknowledgements

This book could not have been written without the numerous research contributions and items of correspondence acknowledged in the notes and references. I must also thank the staff of the various regional development authorities, set up in advance of local government reform, notably North-east Scotland Development Authority (NESDA) and the Highlands and Islands Development Board (HIDB) I am grateful to Mrs May Atherton for her efficient typing, and to both Mr David Orme and Miss Ruth Rowell of the Leicester University Geography Department for their customary cartographic excellence. Finally I thank my wife for her generous assistance and my two sons, to whom this book is dedicated, for their more or less cheerful countenance on the many occasions when family outings degenerated into extended field studies.

Notes and References

References to the (Old) Statistical Account and the New
(Second) Statistical Account, published during the 1790s and
1840s respectively are abbreviated OSA and NSA respectively.
The following abbreviations are also used for journals which
have frequent mention:

EG	Economic Geography	Geog	Geography
GJ	Geographical Journal	IA	Industrial Archaeology
JAE	Journal of Agricultural Economics	JE	Journal of Ecology
		JHG	Journal of Historical Geography
PSAS	Proceedings of the Society of Antiquaries for Scotland	SA	Scottish Agriculture
		SAE	Scottish Agricultural Economics
SF	Scottish Forestry		
SGM	Scottish Agricultural Magazine	SHR	Scottish Historical Review
SS	Scottish Studies	TCP	Town and Country Planning
TDGNHAS	Transactions, Dumfries and Galloway Natural History and Archaeological Society	TESG	Tijdschrift voor Econ en Soc Geografie
		TH	Textile History
		THASS	Transactions, Highland and Agricultural Society of Scotland
TIBG	Transactions, Institute of British Geographers		
		TPR	Town Planning Review

Chapter 1

The Historical Base for Industrial Growth (pages 12-43)

1 Houston, J. M. 'The Scottish Burgh' TPR, 25, 115 (1954);
   for further information see Donaldson, G. Scotland: The
   Shaping of a Nation (Newton Abbot: David & Charles, 1974),
   Smout, T. C. A History of the Scottish People (Edinburgh:
   Collins, 1969)
2 Rampini, C. A History of Moray & Nairn (Edinburgh:
   Blackwood, 1897), 266
3 Muir, R. The Political Geography of North-east Scotland
   (University of Aberdeen: Ph D thesis 1970); see also the
   works of Simpson, W. D. 'The Province of Mar' Aberdeen
   University Studies, 121 and 'The Earldom of Mar', ibid, 124
4 Geddes, A. 'The Royal Four Towns of Lochmaben', TDGNHAS, 39,
   88 (1962)
5 Whitehead, J. P. and Alauddin, K. 'The Town Plans of
   Scotland: Some Preliminary Considerations', SGM, 85, 109
   (1969)
6 Lythe, S. G. E. The Economy of Scotland (Edinburgh: Oliver
   & Boyd, 1960), 38; Rae, T. I. The Administration of the
   Scottish Frontier, 1516-1603 (Edinburgh University Press,
   1966)
7 Smout, T. C. 'The Lead Mines of Wanlockhead' TDGNHAS, 39,
   144 (1962)
8 Grant, I. F. 'An Old Scottish Handicraft Industry', SHR,
   18, 277 (1921)
9 Devine, T.M. and Lythe, S. G. E. 'The Economy of Scotland
   under James VI', SHR, 50, 91 (1971); more specifically see
   Cunningham, A. The Loyal Clans (Cambridge UP, 1932);
   Kermack, W. R. The Scottish Highlands (Edinburgh: Johnston-
   Bacon 1957)
10 Lehmann, W. C. Henry Hume, Lord Kames and the Scottish
   Enlightenment (The Hague: Nijhoff, 1971) XII; see also the
   assessments of Berry, J. James Dunbar 1742-1798: A Study
   of His Thought and of His Contribution to the Scottish
   Enlightenment (London University: Ph D thesis 1970)
   Contemporary conditions are discussed by Emery, F. V. 'A
   Geographical Description of Scotland prior to the Statisti-
   cal Account, SS,3,1(1959); O'Dell 'A View of Scotland in
   the Middle of the Eighteenth Century'SGM, 69, 58 (1953)
   Dickie, J. M. 'The Economic Position of Scotland in 1760',
   SHR, 13, (1920)
11 Caird, J. B. 'The Making of the Scottish Rural Landscape',
   SGM, 80, 72 (1964); Kay, G. 'The Landscape of Improvement:
   A Case Study of Agricultural Change in North-east Scotland',

SGM, 78, 100 (1962); Smout, T. C. 'Scottish Landowners and Economic Growth, 1650-1850', SJPE 11, 218 (1964)

12 Beauties of Scotland, 5, 314; see also Woolmer, H. 'Grantown on Spey: An Eighteenth Century New Town', TPR, 41, 237 (1970)

13 OSA, 6, 129

14 Wood, J. D. 'Planning Intentions for Nineteenth-Century Scottish Estate Village', SS, 15, 51 (1971)

15 OSA, 'Kirkhill (Inverness)', 4, 120

16 Hamilton, H. (ed). Selections from the Monymusk Papers (Edinburgh: Scottish History Society, 1945) 143; Idem (ed). Life and Labour on an Aberdeenshire Estate 1735-1750 (Aberdeen: Third Spalding Club, 1946)

17 For contemporary schemes of Highland development see Cregeen, E. R. 'The Changing Role of the House of Argyll' in Philipson, M. T. and Mitchison, R. (eds). Scotland in the Age of Improvement (Edinburgh UP, 1970); Richards, E. 'The Prospects for Economic Growth in Sutherland at the Time of the Clearances', SHR, 49, 171 (1970)

18 Adam, M. I. 'Eighteenth-century Highland Landlords and the Poverty Problem', SHR, 19, 1 (1926); Carter, I. 'Economic Models and a Recent History of the Highlands, SS, 15, 99 (1971); Youngson, A. J. After the Forty-Five: The Economic Impact on the Scottish Highlands (Edinburgh UP, 1971)

19 Adams, I. H. 'The Historical Geography of Glenfernate, 1460-1968', Scottish Field Studies Association Annual Report 1969, 17 (1970)

20 Numerous local studies are available. See for example Donaldson, G. Northwards by Sea (Edinburgh: John Grant 1966); Haldane, A. R. B. New Ways through the Glens (London: Nelson, 1962); Thomas, J. Regional History of Railways of Great Britain: Scotland (Newton Abbot: David & Charles, 1971)

21 Kyd, J. G. Scottish Population Statistics (Edinburgh: Scottish History Society, 1952); O'Dell, A. C. 'The population of Scotland, 1755-1931: A General Survey', SGM, 48, 282 (1932); Macdonald, D. F. Scotland's Shifting Population, 1770-1850 (Glasgow: Jackson, 1937)

22 Paddison, R. The Evolution and Present Structure of Central Places in North-east Scotland (Aberdeen University: Ph D thesis, 1969)

23 Evenden, L. J. The Settlement Hierarchy in South-east Scotland (Edinburgh University: Ph D thesis, 1969) 281. Local studies include Gibson, R. History of the Town and Parish of Greenlaw (Edinburgh: Oliver & Boyd, 1905)

24 Royal Commission on Local Government 1966-1969 (Wheatley Commission), Report (Edinburgh: HMSO, 1969), Cmnd 4150, Appendices 45

25 Walton, K. 'Population Changes in North-east Scotland
    1696-1951', SS, 5, 149, (1961). Regional trends are also
    examined by Gait, J. M. Aspects of the Population Geography
    of the Eastern Border Counties, 1850-1967 (Edinburgh
    University: Ph D thesis, 1968); Osborne, R. H. 'The Movements
    of People in Scotland 1851-1951', SS, 2, 1 (1958); Soulsby,
    E. M. An Analysis of Selected Aspects of Demographic Change
    in the Border Counties of Scotland, 1755-1961 (St Andrews
    University: Ph D thesis, 1971)
26 Vamplew, W. Railways and the Transformation of the Scottish
    Economy (Edinburgh University: Ph D thesis, 1969)
27 NSA 'Caithness' 15, 56-7
28 Report of the Royal Commission on the Condition of Crofters
    and Cottars in the Highlands and Islands of Scotland
    (Napier Commission), (Edinburgh: HMSO), C 3980
29 Wallace, A. F. 'Forestry Planning on a Highland Estate',
    SF, 17, 49 (1963) Idem 'An Historical Enquiry into Forestry
    on a Highland estate', ibid, 19, 103 (1965)
30 Shorter, A. H. Papermaking in the British Isles: An
    Historical and Geographical Study (Newton Abbot: David &
    Charles, 1971): Thomson, A. G. The Paper Industry in
    Scotland, 1590-1861 (Edinburgh: Scottish Academic Press,
    1974) See also Butt, J. Industrial Archaeology of Scotland
    (Newton Abbot: David & Charles, 1967)
31 OSA, 14, 525
32 Turner, W. H. K. 'The Significance of Water Power in
    Industrial Location', SGM, 74, 98 (1958)
33 OSA, 6, 457
34 Donnachie, I. L. and Stewart, N. R. 'Scottish Windmills:
    An Outline and Inventory', PSAS, 98, 276 (1964-6)
35 Oakley, C. A. Scottish Industry Today: A Survey of Recent
    Developments Undertaken for the Scottish Development Council
    (Edinburgh: Moray Press, 1937)
36 Idem (ed). Scottish Industry: An Account of What Scotland
    Makes and Where She Makes It (Edinburgh: Scottish Council
    Development and Industry, 1955)
37 Snodgrass, C. P. 'Map of Economic Regions of Scotland',
    SGM, 59, 15 (1943); idem 'Recent Population Changes in
    Scotland', ibid, 60, 33 (1944)
38 Linton, D. L. 'Memorandum on the Geographical Factors
    Relevant to the Location of Industry in Scotland, GJ, 92,
    511 (1938). O'Dell, A. C. 'Port Facilities and the
    Dispersal of Industry: The Problem of Scotland, ibid, 97,
    107 (1941)
39 Scottish Economic Committee, The Highlands and Islands of
    Scotland: A Review of the Economic Conditions with
    Recommendations for Improvement (SEC Publication, 1938)

40 Oakley, op cit, 45, (1937). For official Highland policy
    see Scottish Home Department, A Programme of Highland
    Development (Edinburgh: HMSO, 1950), Cmd 7976; Scottish
    Office, Review of Highland Policy (London: HMSO, 1963),
    Cmnd 785; Scottish Office, The Scottish Economy 1965-1970:
    A Plan for Expansion (Edinburgh: HMSO, 1966) Cmnd 2864
41 Data supplied by the Department of Employment, Office for
    Scotland, is gratefully acknowledged

Chapter 2

Textiles: Spread and Specialisation (pages 44-67)

1   OSA, 4, 38
2   OSA, 6, 457
3   Sinclair, J. General Report of the Agricultural State and
    Political Circumstances of Scotland (Edinburgh: np, 1814)
    411
4   NSA, 'Kilmadock', 10, 1239
5   Hamilton, H. The Industrial Revolution in Scotland (Oxford:
    Clarendon Press, 1932), 76; see also Campbell, R. H.
    The Annual Progress of the Linen Manufacture 1727-1754
    (Edinburgh: Scottish Record Office, 1964)
6   Gauldie, E. E. Scottish Bleachfields, 1718-1862 (Queens
    College, University of St Andrews:B Phil thesis, 1967)
7   OSA, 6, 515; see also Turner, W. H. K. The Textile
    Industry of Arbroath since the Early Eighteenth Century
    (Abertay History Society Publication No 2, 1954). The
    cloths were called Osnaburghs after the similarity with the
    Osnabrück product was noticed by a merchant familiar with
    German conditions
8   Cowper, A. S. 'Linen in the Highlands, 1753-1762',
    Edinburgh College of Commerce Occasional Paper, 1 (nd)
9   Turner, W. H. K. 'Flax Cultivation in Scotland: An
    Historical Geography', TIBG, 55, 127 (1972)
10 Gaffney, V. The Lordship of Strathavon (Aberdeen: Third
    Spalding Club, 1960)
11 Bremner, D. The Industries of Scotland: Their Rise,
    Progress and Current Condition (Edinburgh: A. & C. Black,
    1869), 224
12 Ibid, 224-8
13 OSA, 13, 72
14 Gaskin, B. The Decline of the Handloom Weaving Industry in
    Scotland during the Years 1815-1845 (University of
    Edinburgh: Ph D thesis, 1955)
15 NSA, 10, 1124
16 Bremner, op cit 248. See also Gauldie, E. E. (ed). Dundee

Textile Industry, 1790-1885 (Edinburgh: Scottish History Society, 1969); Lenman, B. et al. Dundee and Its Textile Industry, 1850-1914, (Abertay Historical Society Publication, 14, 1969); Turner, W. H. K. 'The Evolution of the Pattern of the Textile Industry within Dundee', TIBG, 18, 107 (1952)

17 Turner, W. H. K. 'Textile Industry of Perth and District', TIBG, 23, 127 (1957)

18 Idem. 'The Concentration of Jute and Heavy Linen Manufactures in East Central Scotland', SGM, 82, 29 (1966); see also Gibson, C. The Story of Jute (Dundee: Museum & Art Gallery, 1959)

19 Marwick, W. H. 'Cotton and the Industrial Revolution in Scotland', SHR, 21, 207 (1924); Mitchell, G. M. 'The English and Scottish Cotton Industries', SHR, 22, 49 (1925)

20 Durie, A. J. 'The Markets for Scottish Linen, 1730-1775', SHR, 52, 49 (1973)

21 Turner, W. H. K. 'Significance of Water Power Sites in Industrial Location', SGM, 74, 98 (1958)

22 Donnachie, I. L. & MacLeod, I. Old Galloway (Newton Abbot: David & Charles, 1974), 83-92, see also Butt, J. 'Industrial Archaeology of Gatehouse of Fleet', IA, 3, 127 (1966)

23 Heron, R. Observations Made in a Journey through the Western Counties of Scotland (Perth: np 1793)

24 OSA, 'Creich (Sutherland)' 8, 374

25 Ibid 377

26 Hamilton, H. Third Statistical Account: Aberdeen (Edinburgh: Oliver & Boyd, 1953), 48

27 General studies of the woollen industry include Martindale, J. G. The Scottish Woollen Industry (International Wool Secretariat, 1954) Turner, W. H. K.'Wool textile industry in Scotland', SGM, 80, 81-9 (1964)

28 On the fortunes of the industry at the time of Union see Campbell, R. H. 'The Economic Consequences of the Anglo-Scottish Union', Economic History Review, 16 (1963-4). Gulvin, C. 'The Union and the Scottish Woollen Industry, 1707-1760', SHR, 50, 121-137 (1971), Smout, T. C. Scottish Trade on the Eve of Union (Edinburgh: Oliver & Boyd, 1963)

29 Martindale, J. G. 'The Rise and Growth of the Tweed Industry in Scotland' in Jenkins, J. G. (ed). The Wool Textile Industry in Great Britain (London: Routledge & Kegan Paul, 1972), 269-80

30 Grant, I. F. 'An Old Scottish Handicraft Industry', SHR 18, 277-89 (1921)

31 For a discussion of the debate on state encouragement in the eighteenth century see Gulvin, C. Scottish Woollen Industry, 1603-1914 (University of Edinburgh: Ph D thesis 1969)

32 OSA, 2, 308
33 The name tweed arises as a corruption of tweel, the traditional name for the weather-resisting cloth of unique texture which was 'twilled in the weave' rendering heavy milling unnecessary. See Oakley. Scottish Industry Today, 59
34 Gulvin, C. The Tweedmakers: A History of the Scottish Fancy Woollen Industry, 1600-1914 (Newton Abbot: David & Charles, 1974); Stillie, T. A. 'The Evolution of Pattern Design in the Scottish Wool-textile Industry in the Nineteenth Century', TH, 1, 309 (1970)
35 Hall, R. History of Galashiels (Galashiels: A. Walker, 1898)
36 MacKinnon, J. The Social and Industrial History of Scotland (London: Longmans Green, 1921), 105
37 Allen, J. R. (ed). Crombies of Grandholm and Cothal, 1805-1960 (Aberdeen: private publication, 1960)
38 Turnbull, J. Hawick in Bygone Days (Hawick: W. & J. Kennedy, 1927). See also Rezaul Hague, A. B. M. Some Geographical Aspects of the Evolution of the Textile Industries in Scotland (University of Edinburgh: M Sc thesis, 1966)
39 Hood, N. 'A Geography of Competition: The Scottish Woollen-textile industry', SGM, 89, 74-80 (1973)
40 Scott, W. R. Home Industries in the Highlands and Islands (Edinburgh: HMSO, 1914), Cd 7564
41 Moisley, H. A.'Harris Tweed: A Growing Highland Industry', EG, 37, 363 (1961); Thompson, F. Harris Tweed (Newton Abbot: David & Charles, 1969). See also the same author's contribution in 1969 on 'Harris Tweed' in the An Comunn Gaidhealach information series (No 16)
42 'Planning for Progress: Shetland Woollen Industry', HIDB Special Report, 4, 197
43 Trade prospects are discussed in M. Gaskin et al. Shetland and the EEC (Aberdeen: University Department of Political Economy, nd), 45-50

Chapter 3

Bladnoch to Highland Park: The Scotch Whisky Record(pages 68-92)

1 Richmond, J. 'Walkers of Aberlour', SM, 101, 365 (1974) deals with another important bakery business.
2 Barnard, A. 'The Whisky Distilleries of the UK' (London: Harpers Gazette, 1887), 181. Reprinted by David & Charles, Glen, I. A. (ed) (1969)
3 Proof strength was deemed as having been reached when gunpowder mixed in whisky flashed on ignition. Since the 1740s, hydrometers have been used and in 1818 under the Hydrometer Act the hydrometer of Bartholomew Sikes was

universally adopted. However, the traditional standard of proof strength remains. The whisky spirit is reduced to 120° for maturation, by the addition of soft water. And for sale the strength is normally brought down further to 70°, although some malts can be obtained at 80 or 85 per cent and it is reported that Clynelish can be found locally in Brora at 96° and Belvenie is bottled at 100°. General information on the industry is given in <u>Scotch Whisky: Questions and Answers</u> (Edinburgh: Scotch Whisky Association nd)

4 The character of different Scotch whiskies is examined by Daiches, D. <u>Scotch Whisky: Its Past and Present</u> (London: Deutsch, 1969). A more elementary guide is provided by Wilson, J. <u>Scotland's Malt Whiskies</u> (Alexandria: Famedram Publishers, 1973)

5 <u>OSA</u>, 'Urquhart (Ross & Cromarty)', 5, 208

6 Youngson, A. J. <u>After the Forty Five</u> (Edinburgh: University Press, 1974), III

7 <u>OSA</u>, 17, 352

8 This followed the Wash Act of 1784 which initiated the distinction between Highland and Lowland, levying a tax of almost 2p per gallon on the wash in the latter area and one of £1 per gallon of still content in the former (with a 20 gallon minimum). Dissatisfaction by the London distillers who could still be undersold in the metropolitan market led to the further legislations two years later. The complicated legal situation in the late eighteenth century is best summarised by Hamilton, J. <u>Economic History of Scotland in the Eighteenth Century</u> (Oxford: Clarendon Press, 1963), 105–110

9 <u>OSA</u>, 4, 122

10 In 1802 duty was payable on each gallon of proof spirit, instead of on still capacity. The rates were set at 19p in the Lowlands and 17p in the Highlands (40p and 33p respectively in 1811). In 1814 the Highland/Lowland distinction was abolished and a uniform rate of 47p imposed. Although lower than the rate in England, that relatively high rate of duty encouraged further illegal operation, especially with a minimum still capacity of 40 gallons now imposed.

11 <u>OSA</u>, 17, 438

12 Bremner <u>The Industries of Scotland</u>, <u>op cit.</u> (Chapter 2 note 11) 447

13 <u>NSA</u>, 13, 135

14 Sillet, S. W. <u>Illicit Scotch</u> (Aberdeen: Impulse Books, 1970)

15 On smuggling see MacDonald, I. <u>Smuggling in the Highlands</u> (Inverness: np, 1914). Some useful photographs and descriptions are included in Thompson, F. 1972 <u>Highland Smugglers</u> (Inverness: Graphis, 1972)

16 Barnard, A. op cit (note 2) 273
17 Teignmouth, Lord, Sketches of the coasts and islands of Scotland (London: J.W. Parker, 1836) 2,378
18 NSA 'Campbeltown (Argyll)' 7,463-4
19 Donnachie, J. Industrial archaeology of Galloway : the regional economy of South West Scotland 1700-1900 (University of Strathclyde : M.Litt. thesis, 1969) 39
20 Black, J. 1870-1 'On the agriculture of Aberdeen and Banff Shires' THASS,   3, 5 (1870-1)
21 NSA 13, 32
22 NSA 10, 328
23 Barnard, A. op cit (note 2) 264
24 Ibid 220
25 Final report of the Royal Commission on whisky and other potable spirits (London : HMSO, 1909) Cd 4876
26 Storrie, M. C.'The Scotch whisky industry', TIBG, 31, 101 (1962
27 Barnard, A. op cit (note 2) 217
28 Storrie, M. C. op cit (note 26) 107
29 The period is examined by Wood, K.'Distilling': Hamilton, H. ed, 1961. The county of Banff (Glasgow : Collins) 111. General references include Dunnett, A. Land of Scotch (Edinburgh : Scotch Whisky Association, 1953); Gunn, N. M. Whisky and Scotland : a political and spiritual survey (London : C. Routledge); Lockhart, R. H. B. Scotch : the whisky of Scotland (London : Putnam, 1965); MacDonald, A. Whisky (Edinburgh : Porpoise Press, 1930); McDowell, J. J. S. Whiskies of Scotland (London: John Murray, 1967)
30 Statistics are drawn from Statistical report for the year 1973 (Edinburgh: Scotch Whisky Association) I am grateful for other information received from the Association and from individual firms covering Edradour, Glenfiddich and Invergordon distilleries. See also Wilson, R, 'The Scotch whisky : the source and nature of statistical information' Journal of the Royal Statistical Society Series A, 1955 345 (1955)
31 Barnard, A. op cit (note 2); Glass, B. W. and Shakerley, C. F. E. Scotch whisky (London: Roger Mortimer & Co, 1973)
32 Macpherson, A.'Scotch whisky', SGM, 80, 99 (1964). A call for the reactivation of the Campbeltown industry was made by Oakley, C. A. Scottish industry today (Edinburgh: Moray Press, 1937) 65
33 Glass, B. W. and Shakerley, C. F. E. op cit (note 31) 3 The business structure of the industry is fully examined by Wilson, R. Scotch: The Formative Years (London: Constable, 1970)
34 The regional situation has been studied by Parham, E. T. Speyside Study (Aberdeen: NESDA, 1973)

35 Storrie, M. C. op cit (note 26) 112
36 Attempts have been made in Australia to imitate Scotch
    whisky using local barley combined with peat and peaty
    water imported from Scotland
37 Hulbert, J. 'Double Trouble for Scotch?', The Scotsman
    (24 June 1972)

Chapter 4

Some Further Industrial Studies (pages 93-123)

1 Smout, T. C. 'The Lead Mines of Wanlockhead', TDGNHAS, 39,
   144 (1962)
2 O'Dell, A. C. The Historical Geography of the Shetland
   Islands (Lerwick: T. and J. Manson, 1939), 167
3 Campbell, W. D. Location Factors in the Development of the
   Scottish iron and steel Industry, 1760-1970 (University of
   Edinburgh: M Sc thesis, 1970)
4 Warren, K. 'Locational Problems of the Scottish Iron and
   Steel Industry since 1760', SGM, 81, 87 (1965)
5 The carbon 'consumption' arises because the cathode in the
   cell is disrupted by the molten cryolite and, unlike the
   'Soderberg' anode which may last more than two years, has
   to be replaced at frequent intervals. The flux is lost by
   waste gases, dust and 'skimmings' from dirty cell baths,
   although in the latter case plant for flux recovery is now
   installed
6 Subsequently renamed British Aluminium Company (BAC). In
   1959 control of the new company was acquired by Tube
   Investments Ltd in association with Reynolds Metal Company,
   USA. Information in this section has been gleaned from
   company publications (including the various editions of
   Aluminium in the Western Highlands) and through correspondence.
   The help of the BAC press and publicity officers, Mr R
   Luckie and his predecessor, Mr P. Bowman, is gratefully
   acknowledged
7 Ingots were imported from the Baie Comeau factory of the
   Canadian British Aluminium Company until the Invergordon
   factory opened.
8 Watts, H. D. 'The Locations of Aluminium Reduction Plant in
   the UK', TESG, 61, 148 (1970)
9 In the other reduction works, process water is a minute
   part of the flow through the power station: up to 700
   million gallons per day at Fort William
10 The History of the British Aluminium Company (London:
   BAC nd), 34
11 Ibid, 19

12 Gregor, M. J. F. and Crichton, R. M. From Croft to Factory: The Evolution of an Industrial Community in the Highlands (Edinburgh: Nelson, 1946), see also Chilton, L. V. 'The Aluminium Industry in Scotland', SGM, 66, 153 (1950)

13 The impact of the Invergordon smelter is discussed in papers by Mackay, G. A. on 'The Economic Impact of a Large-scale Plant on a Remote Area: The Invergordon Smelter' and Drummond, G. G. 'Management Problems of Establishing a Large Plant in a Remote and Rural Area' read at the conference on large-scale developments in remote and rural areas at the University of Aberdeen, March 1973.

14 The versatility of aluminium is increased by alloying with small quantities of copper, manganese, nickel, silicon or zinc and by forms of heat treatment. Aluminium alloys may exceed the strength of mild steel with little more than one third of the weight.

15 Reduction at Rheola (Resolven) and Port Tennant (Swansea) totalled 25,000 ton per annum during the later years of World War II. Rheola is now a rolling mill and Port Tennant is used by a subsidiary company for cable, rod and wire production. Alumina was supplied from a new plant at Newport opened in 1939 (convenient for both labour and bauxite imports) and some of the production was later diverted to Scotland until closure of the works in 1971.

16 Campbell, A. D. and Lyddon, W. D. C. Tayside: Potential for Development (Edinburgh: HMSO, 1970), 110

17 Hamilton, H. 'Industries and commerce' in O'Dell, A. C. and Mackintosh, J. (eds). The North-east of Scotland (Aberdeen: British Association, 1963), 173

18 Bailey, P. Orkney (Newton Abbot: David & Charles, 1971), 150

19 Lythe, S. G. E. 'Gourlays of Dundee: The Rise and Fall of a Scottish Shipbuilding Firm', Abertay History Society Publication, No 10 (1964). Nineteenth-century innovation by Aberdeen shipbuilders is considered by MacGregor, D. R. The Tea Clippers (Lodnon: Conway Maritime Press, 1972)

20 Highland boatbuilding is discussed by Brady, P. 'Fishing: Old Skills Make New Shapes', North 7, No 16, 13 (1973). See also the undated HIDB brochure Fisheries North 7 and data in the RSGS Teacher's Bulletin, No 4, 27

21 Jackson, P. 'Scottish Seaweed Resources', SGM, 64, 137 (1948); Rymer, L. 'The Scottish Kelp Industry', ibid, 90 142 (1974)

22 OSA, 'Stronsay & Eday (Orkney)' 15, 400

23 Donaldson, J. E. Caithness in the Eighteenth Century (Edinburgh: Moray Press, 1938), 149

24 OSA, 'Cross & Burness', 7, 492

25 OSA, 'Orphir', 19, 400

26 Figures quoted by Youngson, A. J. After the Forty Five
    (Edinburgh: University Press, 1974), 135. See also Rampton,
    V. E. Development of the Seaweed Industries in the British
    Isles (Nottingham University: M Sc thesis, 1966)
27 NSA 'Stornoway', 14, 134–5; 'Duirinish (Skye & Lochalsh)',
    14, 194
28 Other constituents include mannitol, which can be used
    as a substitute for sugar in a diabetic diet and incorpor-
    ated in the manufacture of numerous edible and inedible
    products (although high costs limits its application), and
    laminarin, a possible source of glucose
29 In animal feeds, seaweed constitutes up to 10 per cent of
    the material and supplies calcium, carbohydrate, protein,
    trace elements (iodine and iron) and vitamins. See Rampton,
    V. E. 'The Brown Seaweed Industries of the British Isles'
    in Osborne, R. H. et al. (eds). Geographical Essays in
    Honour of K. C. Edwards (Nottingham University Geography
    Department, 1970), 233
30 Booth, E. The Production of Seaweed Meal (Inveresk:
    Institute of Seaweed Research, 1962)
31 It should be explained that alginic acid is a carbohydrate
    and makes up between 15 and 40 per cent of the dry weight
    of seaweed. The crude acid may easily be extracted and then
    combines readily with most metals and organic bases to form
    stable salts. Sodium alginate is most widely used, and from
    the 1880s it was found to be useful as a textile size,
    being introduced into the industry early in the present
    century. However, sodium alginate can be used very widely
    as a thickening and stabilising agent and finds its way
    into a variety of foodstuffs, toiletries, paints and
    pharmaceuticals. Calcium alginate has been put to use in
    the textile industry where alginate fibres, soluble in
    soap and water, are woven in with more delicate fibres to
    allow ease of handling in the manufacture of very light-
    weight fabrics. In addition to published sources, informa-
    tion has been drawn from Alginate Industries and from
    individual collectors.
32 Booth, E. 'Scottish seaweed resources' in Elgood, L. A. et
    al. Natural resources of Scotland (Edinburgh: Scottish
    Council Development and Industry, 1961), 181
33 Information supplied by Mr C. A. Cameron of Alginate
    Industries (Scotland) Ltd is gratefully acknowledged
34 Hume Brown, P. Early Travellers in Scotland (Edinburgh:
    D. Douglas, 1891)
35 Anon. Account of the Pleasure Tours in Scotland (Edinburgh:
    John Thomson, 1824), 182; Itinerary 49
36 There is a notable study of Glenavon deer forest by Gaffney,

V. The Lordship of Strathavon: Tomintoul under the Gordons
(Aberdeen: Third Spalding Club, 1960), 62

37   Scrope, W. The Art of Deer Stalking (London: np, 1838);
     idem. Days of Deer Stalking in the Scottish Highlands
     (London: Hamilton Adams, 1883)

38   Idem. Days and Nights of Salmon Fishing in the Tweed
     (London: np, 1843); see also Calderwood, W. L. The Salmon
     Rivers and Lochs of Scotland (London: Arnold, 1909)

39   Laing, L. Orkney and Shetland: An Archaeological Guide
     (Newton Abbot: David & Charles, 1974)

40   Banks, F. R. Scottish Border Country (London: Batsford,
     1951); Eddington, A. Castles and Historic Houses of the
     Border (Edinburgh: Oliver & Boyd, 1926)

41   I am grateful to the SYHA and the Scottish Tourist Boards
     for providing data

42   HIDB. Fourth Report 1969 (Inverness) 47, (1970), see also
     Scottish Development Department. Cairngorm Area (Edinburgh:
     HMSO, 1967) and earlier studies: Burton, J. H. The
     Cairngorm Mountains (Edinburgh: Blackwood, 1864); Gordon, S.
     The Cairngorm Hills of Scotland (London: Cassell, 1925)

43   Bayfield, N. G. 'Some Effects of Walking and Skiing on
     Vegetation at Cairngorm' in Duffey, E. and Watt, A. S.
     (eds). The Scientific Management of Animal and Plant
     Communities for Conservation (Oxford: Blackwell, 1971)
     469; Nethersole-Thompson, D. and Watson, A. The Cairngorms
     (London: Collins, 1974); Pears, N. V. 'Man in the Cairngorms:
     A population-resource Balance Problem, SGM, 84, 45 (1968)

44   Parnell, B. K. Gairloch – Poolewe : A Study and Plan for
     Recreation and Tourism in Wester Ross (Glasgow School of
     Art: Department of Planning, nd), 11

45   Idem. Aonach Mor: A Planning Report on the Prospect of
     Winter Sport Development at Fort William (Glasgow School of
     Art: Department of Planning, 1974)

46   HIDB First Report 1965/6 (Inverness), 23, 1967

47   HIDB Seventh Report 1972 (Inverness), 38, 1973

48   Area studies include Parnell, B. K. (ed). Lochaber and
     North Argyll (Glasgow School of Art: Department of
     Planning, 1971); Walton, K. (ed). Royal Grampian Country
     (Aberdeen University: Department of Geography, 1969)

49   Scotland,1931, Report of the National Parks Committee
     (London: HMSO) Cmd 3851; Scotland 1945, National Parks: A
     Scottish Survey (Edinburgh: HMSO) Cmd 6631; Scotland 1947,
     National Parks and the Conservation of Nature in Scotland
     (Edinburgh: HMSO) Cmd 7235. An important case study has
     been made of one area: Mather, A. Glenstrathfarrar: Land
     Development Survey (Aberdeen University: Department of
     Geography, 1969). See also Sheail, J. 'The concept of National

Parks in Great Britain' 1900–1950', _TIBG_, 66, 41 (1975)

50 A notable study has been contributed by Brownrigg, M. and
    Greig, M. A. 'The Economic Impact of Tourism Spending in
    Skye', HIDB Special Report 13 (1974)
51 Millman, R. N. Outdoor Recreation in the Highland Country-
    side (University of Aberdeen: Ph D thesis, 1970);
    Wibberley, G. 'Conflicts in the Countryside', TCP, 40, 259
    (1972)

Chapter 5

North Sea Oil and the Impact on Regional Development (pages 124–146)

1   O'Dell, A. C. 'A Century of Coal Transport: Scotland' in
    Stamp, L. D. and Wooldridge, S. W. (eds). London Essays in
    Geography (London: Longmans, 1951) 229
2   Brown, J. The History of Sanquhar (Dumfires: J. Anderson,
    1891), 339–70
3   Discussed by Wood, J. D. The Geography of the Nithsdale-
    Annandale Region, 1813–1816 (University of Edinburgh: Ph D
    thesis, 1962)
4   Lea, K. J. 'Hydroelectric Power Developments and the
    Landscape in the Highlands', SGM, 84, 239 (1965)
5   Scottish Economic Committee, 1938 Highlands and Islands of
    Scotland: A Review of Economic Conditions and Recommenda-
    tions for Improvement (Edinburgh: SEC Publication), 134.
    See also Baily, F. G. 'Water Resources of Scotland', SGM,
    47, 129 (1931)
6   Lea, K. J. 'Hydroelectricity in Scotland', TIBG, 46, 155
    (1961)
7   Hamilton, A. et al. 'Offshore Exploration', Financial Times
    Survey (17 June 1974), 13
8   Considered by Economist Intelligence Unit, 1975 Buchan
    Impact Study (London: EIU), 2 vols. See also Sprott, T.
    'Planning for Rapid Development', The Planner, 60, 846
    (1975)
9   The 'Invergordon Petroleum Saga' is described by Christie,
    D. M. Freight Transport in the Highlands (Dundee University:
    Ph D thesis 1972), Appendix 1
10 Jones, M. R. 'Recent Migration from within Scotland',
    TESG, 58, 135 (1967); Ng, R. 'Internal Migration Regions
    in Scotland', Geografiska Annaler, 51B, 139 (1970)
11 Scottish Office, 1963, Review of Highland Policy (London:
    HMSO). Cmd 7858 see also Scottish Home Department, 1950,
    A programme of Highland Development (Edinburgh: HMSO),
    Cmd 7976
12 Scottish Office, 1966, The Scottish Economy, 1965–1970: A

Plan for Expansion (Edinburgh: HMSO), Cmnd 2864 55. For studies of commuting areas, see Fleming, J. B. and Green, F. H. W. 'Some Relations between Town and Country in Scotland' SGM, 68, 2 (1952); Report of the Royal Commission on Local Government in Scotland (Edinburgh: HMSO), Cmnd 4150, Appendices 45-50

13 Ibid, 150. For a discussion of growth centres in practice see Moseley, M. J. Growth Centres in Spatial Planning (Oxford: Pergamon Press, 1974), 23

14 Ibid, 126. This policy reflects the thinking of the Scottish Economic Planning Committee, 1965, North-east Scotland: A Preliminary Report (Edinburgh: HMSO) 34

15 Gaskin, M. (ed). North-east Scotland: A Survey of its Development Potential (Edinburgh: HMSO, 1969) 19

16 Scottish Council (Development & Industry), 1968, Lochaber Study: Employment Survey, 1966-1981 (Edinburgh: SCDI)

17 Scottish Office, op cit (n 10), 56

18 Scottish Development Department, 1968 The Central Borders (Edinburgh: HMSO); idem, 1970, A Strategy for South-west Scotland (Edinburgh: HMSO). Further material on the Borders is contained in the Peebles, Roxburgh & Selkirk Joint Planning Advisory Committee's promotional brochure on Scottish Border Development and the Borders Regional Planning Unit's Profile of the Borders 1974

19 Campbell, A. D. and Lyddon, W. D. C. Tayside: Potential for Development (Edinburgh: HMSO, 1970); Masser, I. 'Three Estuarine Studies', TPR, 43, 116 (1973)

20 Payne, G. The Tay Valley Plan: A Physical, Social and Economic Survey and Plan for the Future Development of East Central Scotland (1950)

21 Darling, F. F. (ed). West Highland Survey (London: OUP, 1955), 362

22 Advisory Panel on the Highlands and Islands, 1964, Report on Land Use (Edinburgh: HMSO), 2

23 HIDB, 1967, First Report 1965/6 (Inverness), 9. See also Grieve, R. 'Problems and Objectives in the Highlands and Islands' in Ashton, J. and Long, W. H. (eds). The Remoter Rural Areas of Britain (Edinburgh: Oliver & Boyd, 1972), 130

24 HIDB, 1971, Fifth Report 1970 (Inverness), 19

25 Gaskin, M. in the Evening Express (Aberdeen) May 1969, 5.

26 NESDA, 1972, Report for 1971-2 (Aberdeen), 5

27 Nicoll, R. E. et al. A Future for Scotland: A Study of the Key Factors Associated with Growth in Scotland (Edinburgh: Scottish Council Development & Industry, 1973) 10-11

28 Ibid, 17

29 Select committee on Scottish Affairs, 1972, Land Resource Use in Scotland (Edinburgh: HMSO) Cmnd 5226, 1, 15

30 Aberdeen County Council Planning Department, 1972, <u>Deer District Strategic Plan</u> (Aberdeen); Idem, 1973, <u>Buchan: The Next Decade</u> (Aberdeen); Berwickshire Planning Office, 1972, <u>A Rural Policy for Berwickshire</u> (Duns)

31 Hutchinson, P. G. <u>Rural Growth Centres Policy of the Highlands and Islands of Scotland</u> (University of Glasgow: B Phil thesis, 1969); Parham, E. T. <u>Speyside Study</u> (Aberdeen: NESDA, 1973). General studies include Gaskin, M. <u>The Economic Impact of North Sea Oil on Scotland</u> (Edinburgh: Royal Bank of Scotland, 1973); Mackay, D. I. and Mackay, G. A. <u>The Political Economy of North Sea Oil</u> (London: Martin Robertson, 1975); Walmsley, P. J. et al. <u>North Sea Oil and Gas: The Challenge and the Implications</u> (Edinburgh: Heriot-Watt University, 1973). See also Ardern, R. J. 'No Slick Answers?: Library Resources to Serve the Offshore Oil Industry' <u>Aslib Proceedings</u> 27,173 (1975); Social Science Research Council, 1975, <u>Research into the Social Impact of North Sea Oil Developments in Scotland</u> (London: SSRC)

32 Rural studies of the islands include Coull, J. R. 'The Economic Development of the Island of Westray, Orkney', <u>SGM</u>, 82, 154 (1966). Miller, R. and Luther-Davies, S. <u>Eday & Hoy: A Development Survey</u> (Glasgow University: Department of Geography, 1968); Grimond, L. 'Rural Revival in Hoy', <u>TCP</u>, 42, 366 (1914)

33 Baur, C. et al. 'North-east Scotland', <u>Financial Times Report</u> (17 May 1974), 15

34 Economic and Planning Consultants, 1974 (Edinburgh: Bell Lawrie Robertson)

35 North-east Scotland Joint Planning Advisory Committee, 1974, <u>The Regional Report: Function and Uses: Summary and Conclusions</u> (Aberdeen), 26

36 Scottish Development Department, 1972, <u>The Size and Distribution of Scotland's Population: Projections for Planning Purposes</u> (Edinburgh: HMSO), 22

37 Scottish Development Department, 1973, <u>North Sea Oil: Production Platform Towers: Construction Sites: Discussion Paper</u> (Edinburgh); Idem, 1974, <u>North Sea Oil and Gas: Coastal Planning Guidelines</u> (Edinburgh). For discussion see Turnock, D. 'The Impact of Oil Discoveries on the Scottish Highlands and Islands', <u>TCP</u>, 43, 12 (1975)

38 Baur, C. et al. 'Scotland', <u>Financial Times Survey</u> (11 November 1974) 23

39 North-east Scotland Joint Planning Advisory Committee, 1972, <u>Housing in the Aberdeen Area</u> (Aberdeen), 33

40 Gaskin, M. op cit (n 15), 24

41 Jack Holmes Planning Group, 1968, <u>The Moray Firth: A Plan for Growth in a Subregion of the Scottish Highlands</u>

(Inverness: HIDB). The same group produced a development
plan for Sutherland in 1973, and a Dornoch Firth Study was
produced by the University of Edinburgh Department of
Urban and Regional Studies in the same year. See also
Smith, J. S. 'Development and Rural Conservation in Easter
Ross', SGM, 90, 42 (1974)

42 Ross & Cromarty County Planning Department, 1973,
Development Plan: Report and Policy Statement (Dingwall)
Clark, I. R. 'Shetland Oil: Round One' in The Highland
Fund 1973-4 (Annual Report, 1974), 8

43 Warren, A. and Harrison, C. M. 'A Proposed Nature
Conservation Plant for Shetland' (University College,
London, Discussion Papers in Conservation, 1974), 7. See
also Francis, J. and Swan, N. Scotland in Turmoil (Edinburgh:
St Andrews Press, 1973); Gaskin, M. 'The Remoter Rural
Areas in the National Context' in Ashton and Long, op cit
(n 21), 165; Nicholson, J. R. Shetland and Oil (London:
William Luscombe, 1975)

44 Broady, M. 'The Drumbuie Inquiry: David and Goliath in
Scottish Rural Development', Community Development Journal,
10, 79, (1975)

45 Scottish Development Department, op cit (n 37)

46 HIDB, 1967, First Report 1965-6 (Inverness), 5

47 Relevant literature includes Gaskin, M. Freight Rates and
Prices in the Islands (Inverness: HIDB, 1971); Skewis, W. I.
Transport in the Highlands and Islands (Glasgow University:
Ph D thesis, 1962)

48 Turnock, D. 'Depopulation in North-east Scotland with
Reference to the Countryside', SGM, 84, 256 (1968)

49 Ardern, R. J. and Carter, M. P. (eds). North of Scotland
Register of Research in the Social Sciences (Aberdeen
University: Department of Sociology, 1974)

Index

aluminium industry in 95-102
see also Lochaber

Galashiels 36 39 41 54-57 135
Galloway see Dumfries &
  Galloway
Gatehouse of Fleet 51-52
Glass industry 13 108
Grampian region 16 19 28-30 77
  79 103 116
  North Sea oil in 138 141-142
  planning in 134-136
  textile industry in 44 47 57
  see also individual towns and
  sub-regions
Granite industry 24 28 30 102
Grantown on Spey 14
Growth points 32 133-136 146

Harris 61-62
Harris Tweed 61-62
Hawick 18-19 55-56 58
Hebrides see Western Isles and
  individual islands
Hemp see Textiles
Highland Fund 141
Highland Panel 134
Highland policy 14 16 134-136
  see also Highlands and
  Islands Development Board
Highland region 18-19 30 120
  industry in 22-23 47-48 52
  66-79   94-102 109-113
  planning in 134-136
Highlands and Islands Develop-
  ment Board 60 82 93 107
  120-125 133-135 143-145
Hill farming 99
Home industry see Domestic
  industry
Hosiery see Textiles
Hotels 120
Huntly 28 33 36 89 103 133
Hydroelectricity 30 95-97
  126-128

Imperial Chemical Industries
  108
Industry see individual

industries
diversification of 146
impact of 98-99 133 141-145
linkage of 89
spread of 19 138 see also
  Diffusion of industry and
  Growth points
Inverness 32-33 36 133 144
  industry in 54 60 84
Invergordon 88 97-102 136 138
  143-144
Inverurie 103 143
Iron industry 18 93-94
Islands see individual islands
Islay 24 30 93
  whisky distilling in 70 78-79
  84 88-89 91 116

Jute see Textiles

Keith 28 57 103 133
Kelp 109 110
Kincardine & Deeside 48 113
Kintyre 32 75 111
Kirkwall 107 116 133 144
Kyle of Lochalsh 144-145

Labour catchments 133 136
Labour shedding 138
Labour supply see Employment
Langholm 12 56
Lerwick 33-36 63-64 131 133
Lewis 61-62 77 136 144
Light industry 18-19 103 132
  see also individual industries
Lime industry 24
Linen see Textiles
Linkages see Industry
Lochaber 110 112 125-126 133
  see also Fort William
Lossiemouth 105-108

Male employment 39-41
Malting 69 84
Marine engineering 28 104-107
Marine services 142
Metallic ores 30 93
Metallurgy 93-102
Migration see Population
Milk manufacture 25-26